Around the Circle Gently

Quotations about

Birth, Families, Life

Compiled and edited by

Lynn Moen & Judy Laik

Book Publishers Network

Book Publishers Network
PO Box 2256
Bothell, WA 98041

LCCN 2010911143

ISBN 10   1-935359-50-9
ISBN 13   978-1-935359-50-0

10 9 8 7 6 5 4 3 2 1

First edition, 1995
Second edition, 2011

Cover design: John Moen
Text design: Judy Laik and Lynn Moen

Contents

Introduction
to the Second Edition - 2011

In *Around the Circle Gently,* the quotations are
arranged to give you a feeling of sitting in on a
conversation between famous (and not-so-famous)
people with their own views on the topics of love,
families, and life. The wisdom and gentle humor can
offer inspiration and pleasure for today's busy lives.

Over fifteen years have gone by since the book was
first published. It's been out of print for several years, and
we are glad to offer it again, both to its fans from the
initial publication and to others who aren't yet
acquainted with its specialness.

We have reformatted the book, eliminated a few
quotes that no longer seemed relevant to today, and
included additional material. Working with these words
reminded us again of the world's great store of insight,
knowledge, guidance, and amusement, and that a
beautifully expressed sentiment is never stale.

Lynn Moen & Judy Laik

aroundthecirclegently.com

Introduction
to the First Edition -1995

No matter what else one does in life, the most important and enduring thing most of us do is to raise a family—important, but not always easy. If we came from a happy family, how we were raised can serve as a good example for us as parents. However, if the family we came from was less than ideal, we may seek a better path to follow, for the sake of both our children and ourselves.

To find this better path, we need encouragement and empathy, ideas and inspiration—perhaps an occasional laugh—to give us perspective and help us feel less alone. Our collection of quotations, quips, and wise sayings represents the best thought we have come across on different aspects of family life: pregnancy and birth; raising children; being a parent; our relationships with our spouses, our families, and others we love; the "golden years" after our children are grown; and, inevitably, coming to grips with old age and death.

Of course there is no "one right way" in childrearing, nor in any human relationship. Often what we need is not the "right" answer, but to hear there *are* answers. Each of us needs to find ways that work for our unique family. It is our hope that in these pages you will find signposts as you follow your own best path.

We have always been fascinated by words and their power, appreciating the various ways different people will express a thought: poetically, succinctly, or with humor. After all the years we've worked with words and books, separately and together, we still have a "Wow" feeling when we come across an idea expressed in a particularly felicitous way. This book was a natural outgrowth of our fascination.

Lynn Moen and Judy Laik

Dedication

To **Morris**, my husband, friend and partner,
who has been such a wonderful
husband and father to our children.
And to **Martha**, her husband, **Scott**,
their daughters, **Miranda** and **Laura**,
And to **Keith**, his wife, **Barbara**,
his son **Henry** and daughter **Sofia**,
her son **Conner**,
and their daughter **Katie**.
And to **Arne**, his wife , **Colleen**,
their sons **Jake** and **Brody**.
And to **John**, his wife **Kim**,
their son **Xavier** and daughter **Kaia**.
I love you all.
(Lynn Moen)

As always, to my husband **Rein**, still my best friend
and traveling companion through life,
to our children: **Jeff**, his wife **Beth**; **Rani**; and **Jennifer**;
our grandchildren:
Becca, **Brett**, **Candis**, **Brendan**, and **Emilie**;
and to great-grandson **Ricky**,
and a new great-grandson,
due some time near Christmas.
(Judy Laik)

Beginnings
Love

Love is that condition in which the happiness of another person is essential to your own.

- ROBERT A. HEINLEIN

True love comes quietly, without banners or flashing lights. If you hear bells, get your ears checked.

- ERICH SEGAL

Love does not consist in gazing at each other, but in looking together in the same direction.

- ANTOINE de SAINT-EXUPÉRY

Through loving each other as we did, we offered a mirror, one to the other, through which to see ourselves in whole new ways.

- CAROL LEMIEUX

The supreme happiness of life is the conviction of being loved for yourself, or, more correctly, being loved in spite of yourself.

- VICTOR HUGO (19th century)

In real love you want the other person's good. In romantic love you want the other person.

- MARGARET ANDERSON

No partner in a love relationship should feel that he has to give up an essential part of himself to make it viable.

- MAY SARTON

Selfishness is not living as one wishes to live but asking others to live as one wishes to live.

- OSCAR WILDE

Marriage

You make what seems a simple choice: choose a man or a job or a neighborhood—and what you have chosen is not a man or a job or a neighborhood, but a life.

- JESSAMYN WEST

Marriage is not just spiritual communion and passionate embraces; marriage is also three meals a day, sharing the workload and remembering to carry out the trash.

- JOYCE BROTHERS

After ecstasy, the laundry.

- ZEN SAYING

Formal courtesy between husband and wife is even more important than it is between strangers.

- ROBERT A. HEINLEIN

Success in marriage is much more than finding the right person; it is being the right person.

- OLD SAYING

One must relinquish the hope of creating the perfect partner before one can genuinely love the real one.

- EVELYN BASSOFF

Every young girl marries believing that she will change her groom for the better, every young man marries believing that his bride will never change, and both are inevitably disappointed.

- GEORGE BERNARD SHAW

The only time a woman really succeeds in changing a man is when he's a baby.

- NATALIE WOOD

The ultimate test of a relationship is to disagree but to hold hands.

- ALEXANDRA PENNEY

A marriage without conflicts is almost as inconceivable as a nation without crises.

- ANDRÉ MAUROIS

A happy marriage is the union of two good forgivers.

- ROBERT QUILLEN

Love is an act of endless forgiveness, a tender look which becomes a habit.

- PETER USTINOV

In a successful marriage, there is no such thing as one's way. There is only the way of both, only the bumpy, dusty, difficult, but always mutual path!

- PHYLLIS McGINLEY

A successful marriage is not a gift, it is an achievement.

- ANN LANDERS

Chains do not hold a marriage together. It is threads, hundreds of tiny threads, which sew people together through the years.

- SIMONE SIGNORET

Why do fairy tales always end with the prince and princess marrying? . . . Did Cinderella ever wake up in the morning to the cry of her baby, feeling as evil and fussy as her stepsisters?

- ANGELA BARRON McBRIDE

Conception

Literature is mostly about having sex and not much about having children. Life is the other way around.

- DAVID LODGE

Making the decision to have a child — it's momentous. It is to decide forever to have your heart go walking around outside your body.

- ELIZABETH STONE

[Being a parent] is tough. If you just want a wonderful little creature to love, you can get a puppy.

- BARBARA WALTERS

There is no commitment that two people can make that is as binding and exciting as choosing to have a baby together. It's miraculous when the love of two beings creates a third.

- JOY GARDNER

Babies are such a nice way to start people.

- DON HEROLD

Babies And Other Hazards Of Sex: How to make a tiny person in only 9 months, with tools you probably have around the home.

- DAVE BARRY, book title

Have children while your parents are still young enough to take care of them.

- RITA RUDNER

The nurse, very soberly, said that my test result was 'strongly positive.' I immediately felt, 'Good for you, little baby! You are not apologetically tip-toeing into this world. You are, after all, Strongly Positive!'

- JUDY SANDERS

4

Pregnancy

The two most beautiful sights I have witnessed in my life are a full blown ship at sail and the round-bellied pregnant female.

- BENJAMIN FRANKLIN (1706-1790)

Pay attention to the pregnant woman! There is no one more important than she!

- CHAGGA SAYING, Africa

The street's abloom with pregnant women. They stand next to me in elevators. I see them on movie lines, getting out of taxicabs. . . . Were they here before I was pregnant?

- PHYLLIS CHESLER

Pregnancy is your time, . . . a transition stage that enables you to grow into parenthood. . . . You have nine months in which to slowly grow, evolve, nourish, sustain, and ultimately give birth to a new life.

- SYLVIA KLEIN OLKIN

Being pregnant is like getting on a train that whisks you down the track to a destination not precisely known.

- RAHIMA BALDWIN

Pregnancy is . . . a roller coaster ride of hopes, dreams, love and emotional adjustments from the time the pregnancy is established until the baby is born.

- VICKI WALTON

Pregnancy is a time of being in touch with the power of creation itself.

- RAHIMA BALDWIN

Pregnancy is a contradiction. It is a time of daydreams, fantasies and expectations. But it is also a time of inward searching, inward dwelling, and inward exploration.

- SYLVIA KLEIN OLKIN

Pregnancy can be a time of personal (not just fetal) growth and a precious, heightened phase in a woman's life.

- ELIZABETH DAVIS

My husband would say to me, 'Aren't pregnant women supposed to be radiant? When are you going to be radiant?' And I'd say, 'When I stop throwing up.'

- K. C. COLE

The biggest problem facing a pregnant woman is not nausea or fatigue or her wardrobe — it's free advice.

- SOPHIA LOREN

Life is tough enough without having someone kick you from the inside.

- RITA RUDNER

Being pregnant . . . is not much of a secret once your belly beats you through the door.

- LESLIE LEHR SPIRSON

Allegedly, there are hordes of men who are wildly attracted to pregnant women. You will have to spend much of your pregnancy fending off their advances. The only question is: Where are these men anyway?

- RUTH PENNEBAKER & LIBBY WILSON

Expectant Fathers

Parenting begins with conception, not childbirth.

- JACK R. HEINOWITZ

When a couple . . . share in . . . the experience of
pregnancy and childbirth, the husband's involvement
enhances the alliance that has already been formed. They
see their relationship in a new light, and enter a new
phase of life together.

- ARTHUR & LIBBY COLMAN

Face it — you're as pregnant as your wife.

- BILL M. ATALLA

As pregnancy progresses and men feel their child's
'presence,' they begin to see themselves differently — not
so much as sons but as fathers.

- JACK R. HEINOWITZ

I realized later that my wife's complaints [in the late
months of pregnancy] were actually cries for sympathy,
and a few kind words of encouragement from me would
have been greatly appreciated.

- BILL M. ATALLA

Men often find themselves playing two roles; roles that
are contradictory. They find that they must be
understanding and not pressure their wives into having
sex, while at the same time they must transmit the
message, and do it subtly, that they still find their wives
incredibly exciting.

- RANDY MEYERS WOLFSON & VIRGINIA DeLUCA

You are pregnant because he wanted you. In all the fuss,
don't forget that. He still wants you.

- LESLIE LEHR SPIRSON

Preparing for Birth

Lessons in preparing for childbirth are lessons in living.
- LYNN MOEN

Because our society has long shrouded birth in mystery,
women have no opportunity to observe the reality of
birth before they, themselves, have their babies. . . . She is
venturing into *terra incognita* with a second-hand travel
guide in her head which is incomplete at best, and at
worst colors her experience of birth in terrifying hues.
- LESTER DESSEZ HAZELL

Most fears thrive in ignorance.
- SYLVIA KLEIN OLKIN

When my doctor saw my Birth Plan, she said, 'You've
been reading books!'
I replied, laughing, 'Don't you?'
She countered, 'It's my job.'
'Well,' I said, 'having a baby is mine at the moment —
and I want to do it as well as I can.'
- SHEILA KITZINGER quoting an expectant mother

The more you prepare your body, your spirit, and your
mind, the easier [birth] will be. . . . because it is something
that happens to you, it is not something that you do. It
takes a lot of will power and control to let your body do
what it needs to do.
- NAN KOEHLER

Planning for birth is like getting ready for an athletic
event. . . . You can't predict exactly what is going to
happen; the events of the game will unfold according to
their own particular logic, and not necessarily according
to your plan.
- ADRIENNE LIEBERMAN

Anticipating Birth

Three months dreary,
Three months cheery,
Three months weary.

- OLD SAYING about pregnancy

Everything, everywhere, with the exception of reproduction, seems geared to the frantic jet age. No amount of doing can trim time off those necessary ten lunar months to produce a healthy, full term baby.

- MARGARET GAMPER

In pregnancy the body parks itself in the middle of your mind and won't budge.

- MARNI JACKSON

[Being pregnant is] getting company inside one's skin.

- MAGGIE SCARF

I've begun to love this little creature and to anticipate his birth as a fresh twist to a knot which I do not wish to untie.

- MARY WOLLSTONECRAFT (1797-1851)

MOTHERHOOD . . . waiting is the hardest part.

- TEE-SHIRT

It is a wonder to carry inside you someone else's body; . . . to see [it] at last; . . . to watch it nurse at your breast till you almost know it better than yourself — better than it knows itself.

- RANDALL JARRELL

Childbirth calls into question our very existence, requiring an expectant couple to confront not only new life but death, pain, fear, and, most of all, change.

- ELIZABETH NOBLE quoting a new mother

Midwives & Support

The goats have no midwives.
The sheep have no midwives.
When the goat is pregnant she is safely delivered.
When the sheep is pregnant she is safely delivered.
You, in this state of pregnancy, will be safely delivered.

- AFRICAN YORUBA CHANT of the village midwife and elders

The midwife informs, teaches, and allows the magical
powers of trust and caring to envelop the family, the
mother, and the infant. The root of caring is to respect
the rhythms, needs, and abilities of another.

- MARY C. HOWELL, M.D.

Women have always been healers. . . . They were
midwives, travelling from home to home. . . . They were
called 'wise women' by the people, witches or charlatans
by the authorities. Medicine is part of our heritage as
women, our history, our birthright.

- BARBARA EHRENREICH & DEIRDRE ENGLISH

Birth outcomes are much better in countries — like
Sweden, Holland, and the United Kingdom — where
midwives dramatically outnumber obstetricians and
where midwifery is a well-established profession.

- MICHEL ODENT, M. D.

Midwifery is a vocation, a romance, an addiction, a
religion. It isn't something you dabble in; there's a part of
yourself, of your life, that you give away.

- FRAN VENTRE, midwife

The family's trust in the midwife and the midwife's trust
in the competence of the family members are the basis of
caring that has the power of magic.

- MARY C. HOWELL, M.D.

The midwife cannot be skilled without being caring. She cannot be truly caring without being skilled.

- SHEILA KITZINGER

The better the obstetrician, the more like a midwife he or she becomes.

- NANCY WAINER COHEN

To coach a woman through her labor is to practice the art of kindness in its highest form.

- LESTER DESSEZ HAZELL

The greatest joy is to become a mother; the second greatest is to be a midwife.

- NORWEGIAN PROVERB

'I thought the best husbands looked on their wives' lying-in as a time of festival and jollity. What! Did you not even get drunk in the time of your wife's delivery? Tell me honestly how you employed yourself at this time.' 'Why then honestly,' replied he, 'and in defiance of your laughter, I lay behind her bolster and supported her in my arms.'

- HENRY FIELDING (1707-1756)

The husband is the best medication for relieving pain.

- ROBERTO CALDEYRO-BARCIA

I can certainly sympathize with a father who doesn't want to be a witness to the pain of labor, or who is frightened by hospitals and wary of birth: all that blood and gore. . . . That's exactly how most mothers feel. The difference is, most mothers don't have a choice.

- K.C. COLE

A man doesn't need to be a miracle worker to play his role to perfection. *He merely needs to be there.*

- DALE CLARK

Father's presence serves two purposes. One is to reduce the anguish of the mother. The other is to increase the anguish of the father. Both seem to me laudable goals.

— CHARLES KRAUTHAMMER

The incredible experience of watching your wife labor, helping her breathe, and seeing the beautiful miracle of a new life emerging is almost overwhelming.

— KEN DRUCK

No matter how arduous or painful a man's experience with childbirth may have been, he was profoundly and unequivocally grateful to have been included in this life-changing event.

— TIM SPACEK

The best time of my life has been the three instances where I have been there for the birth of my children. That is, nothing [else] has ever come close.

— STEVEN SPIELBERG

Every woman needs a loving, sharing partner during and after pregnancy, whether or not she has a husband.

— SHEILA KITZINGER

My 'job' is a handholder. Back rubber. Brow wiper. Basin holder. Hall walker. Picture taker. Encourager. Actually this description sounds like a — you guessed it — *mother*.

— SUSAN CAREY, childbirth educator, doula

Labor

It can't possibly be time yet! I'm just a kid! I can only pant for twenty-six seconds. I'm simply not ready. The baby is easier for me to carry around now. I wonder if I could go for ten months instead of nine.

- SUZANNE ARMS

There is no way out of the experience except through it, because it is not really your experience at all but the baby's. Your body is the child's instrument of birth.

- PENELOPE LEACH

The experience of bearing a child is central to a woman's life. Years after the baby has been born she remembers acutely the details of her labour and her feelings as the child was delivered.

- SHEILA KITZINGER

Native American women believe that a laboring woman must leave her body and reach into the stars to bring her baby's spirit safely to Earth through birth.

- JILLIAN VanNOSTRAND

It is not 'ladylike' to give birth. The strength and power of labor is not demure.

- GAYLE PETERSON quoting a midwife

Loss of modesty is a reliable sign of the advent of the second stage.

- KIRSTEN EMMOTT

I ask Laurie if there was any pain and she says, 'No pain, but I know what the Earth feels like making a mountain.'

- ALLEN COHEN

These pains seemed to come . . . like breakers at the seashore. The moment they stopped, you felt . . . ready to dance, only to change your mind rather quickly when the next breaker came.

- MARIA von TRAPP

Women today rely on the props of drugs, machines and other people instead of relying on themselves and their bodies to do the work of labor.

- DIONY YOUNG

Labor can be painful, exhausting, and still euphoric. . . . women who give birth without anesthesia suffer more pain than anesthetized women do, but they also experienced greater pleasure.

- DIANA KORTE & ROBERTA SCAER

Rain, after all is only rain; it is not bad weather. So also, pain is only pain; unless we resist it, when it becomes torment.

- I CHING

With stronger contractions, Lee Ann discovered it helped if she yelled, 'Out! Out! I want you out!' She was referring to the baby and was surprised when her friends quickly left the room.

- ELIZABETH REDDITT-LYON

When Hope went into labor and hit transition she yelled at her midwife: 'What are my options?' 'You don't have any options,' said the midwife. Hope said that helped.

- MIRIAM SAGAN

I discovered I always have choices and sometimes it's only a choice of attitude.

- JUDITH M. KNOWLTON

Giving Birth

Giving birth is an awesome experience. At times it can be emotionally and physically overwhelming. . . . You are both taking part in a miracle as great as the creation of the earth.
- CARL JONES

Childbirth is a much more sensual, emotional, and bonding experience than any teacher or book can convey.
- PATRICK FARENGA

Birth is not one act. It is a process.
- ERICH FROMM

I became convinced that birth, far from being a 'medical problem,' was in fact an integral part of sexual and emotional life
- MICHEL ODENT, M.D.

Birth, like love, is an energy and a process, happening within a relationship. Both unfold with their own timing, with a uniqueness that can never be anticipated, with a power that can never be controlled, but with an exquisite mystery to be appreciated.
- ELIZABETH NOBLE

Strongly felt . . . in all births that I have been a part of is the tension, the excitement, the fear — 'the holding of one's breath.' We may not call it the 'birthforce' but we know what it is when we feel it.
- VANGIE BERGUM

There is power that comes to women when they give birth. They don't ask for it, it simply invades them. Accumulates like clouds on the horizon and passes through, carrying the child with it.
- SHERYL FELDMAN

Birth is very much a body process . . . that seems to work best with the woman integrating her consciousness with her body, as a vine climbs a fence row.

- LEWIS MEHL

Childbirth is more admirable than conquest, more amazing than self-defense, and as courageous as either one.

- GLORIA STEINEM

Birth goes best if it is not intruded upon by strange people and strange events. It goes best when a woman feels safe enough and free enough to abandon herself to the process.

- PENNY ARMSTRONG & SHERYL FELDMAN

Human beings are mammals. All mammals hide themselves, isolate themselves to give birth. They need privacy. It is the same for humans. We should always be aware of this need for privacy.

- MICHEL ODENT, M.D.

Those who still maintain that anesthesia should be used during delivery can never have seen the face of a woman who has herself brought her child into the world.

- FERNAND LAMAZE

Ah, what an incomparable thrill. . . . The sheer pleasure of the feeling of a born baby on one's thighs is like nothing on earth.

- MARGARET DRABBLE

Biologically, you are designed to receive great pleasure from your body not only during lovemaking and intercourse, but in birth and breastfeeding, too. This pleasure — *not duty* — is the best glue for happy families.

- DIANA KORTE & ROBERTA SCAER

Just as the energy of sexual arousal requires surrender if orgasm is to occur, so the energy of birth requires surrender if the baby is going to come out without intervention.

- RAHIMA BALDWIN & TERRA PALMARINI

Birth is no more 'dangerous' than conception . . . . It may be more painful than conception, but, in most situations, it can be just as pleasurable.

- NANCY WAINER COHEN

Birth is as safe as life gets.

- HARRIETTE HARTIGAN

Givng birth is a major event in a woman's life. It can be fulfilling and lead to enhanced self-esteem, or it can leave bitterness or unresolved emotions that last a lifetime.

-- RAHIMA BALDWIN

Childbirth isn't something that is done to you, or for you; it is something you do yourself. Women give birth. Doctors, hospitals, and nurses don't.

- LESTER DESSEZ HAZELL

They shouted and I shouted — not because it was painful but because something elemental and stupendous was happening and I was in on it. And then she was there and I saw her, rosy and perfect. I felt as if I could move mountains. . . . Words cannot recreate this moment. It was one of ecstasy.

- LEONORE PELHAM FRIEDRIECH

The birth of a baby is an everyday miracle — part of a day's work for the doctor, midwife, or nurse, but a deep and permanent memory to the birthing woman and those who love her and support her.

- PENNY SIMKIN

Cesareans

Sometimes in our quest for the perfect birth, we forget that there is no perfect childbirth.

- DEE ALLEN-KIRKHOUSE

Having a Cesarean is Having a Baby.

- DIANA KORTE & ROBERTA SCAER, chapter title

Grapefruits are sectioned, but women give birth.

- RUTH ALLEN

If we perceive that our child is in danger, we will do anything to protect her. . . . We will permit ourselves *to be cut open* to save the life of our baby.

- NANCY WAINER COHEN & LOIS J. ESTNER

The most common cause of cesareans today is not fetal distress or maternal distress, but obstetrician distress.

- GERALD STOBER

The cesarean is not 'easier' for anyone, except the doctor.

- MORTIMER ROSEN, M.D. & LILLIAN THOMAS

Who else goes home a few days after major surgery and has to get up twice a night and take care of a baby?

- BETH SHEARER

In spite of what they have been through — the major surgery, the physical pain, the grieving — cesarean mothers cope. They learn to mother their babies. They heal and often go on to have another baby.

- ROBERTA SCAER

Resolution

What makes a good birth experience [depends on] how
we discover that energy and enthusiasm that carry us
through any challenging situation in life.

- SUZANNE ARMS

Everything worked out fine. We ended up with an
extremely healthy, organic, natural baby, who
immediately demanded to be put back into the uterus.

- DAVE BARRY

All events, except childbirth, can be reduced to a heap of
trivia in the end.

- ANNE TYLER

[After giving birth] all women must have a time of
recollection to piece together all parts of the birthing
experience, which must seem like a jig-saw puzzle. It is
important to remember the passion — the light and dark
of it — and to order it.

- SHEILA KITZINGER

Nature goes on repeating itself but there is no end to its
infinite variety and every spring is a resurrection, every
birth a new beginning. Especially when that new birth is
intimately connected with us, it becomes a revival of
ourselves and our hopes centre around it.

- JAWAHARLAL NEHRU

I would like my children to be the happy ending of my
story.

- MARGARET ATWOOD

Infancy
Babies Are . . .

A baby is God's opinion that the world should go on.
Never will a time come when the most marvelous recent
invention is as marvelous as a newborn baby.
                                        - CARL SANDBURG

There was a star danced and under that was I born.
                                - WILLIAM SHAKESPEARE

The child in the womb sang, 'Let me remember who I
am.' And his first cry after birth was, 'Oh, I have
forgotten.'
                                        - HINDU STORY

The infant that is born on earth brings with it the air of
heaven. In its expression, in its smiles, even in its cry you
hear the melody of the heavens.
                                - HAZRAT INAYAT KHAN

After pointing my camera so many times at the deep blue
gaze of newborns, I see why midwives call them 'fresh
from God.' . . . Their ageless little faces can show us who
we really are by reminding us of our original selves.
                                - MARY MOTLEY KALERGIS

You see, Wendy, when the first baby laughed for the first
time, its laughter broke into a thousand pieces, and they
all went skipping about, and that was the beginning of
fairies.
                                        - J. M. BARRIE

Our attitude toward the newborn child should be one of
reverence that a spiritual being has been confined to
within limits perceptible to us.
                                - MARIA MONTESSORI

When you're drawing up your list of life's miracles, you might place near the top the first moment your baby smiles at you.

- BOB GREENE

A comfortable, happy baby starts smiling goofy little smiles in his sleep when he is just a few days old. His face looks unmistakably happy, and I just don't believe the misguided soul who decided for all of us that these smiles are caused by gas.

- LESTER DESSEZ HAZELL

How can you quarrel with a newborn baby who has stretched out his little arms for you to pick him up?

- MARIA von TRAPP

How delicate the skin, how sweet the breath of children!
- EURIPIDES

The first cry of a newborn baby in Chicago or Zamboango, in Amsterdam or Rangoon, has the same pitch and key, each saying, 'I am! I have come through! I belong!'

- CARL SANDBURG

Life is a flame that is always burning itself out, but it catches fire again every time a child is born.

GEORGE BERNARD SHAW

She blinks her newborn eyes open and looks at you. With that look you know, you just know, . . . as long as you live, you will never *not* care what happens to this person.

- PADDY O'BRIEN

How can he be three months old when he was just born yesterday, and we've had him forever?

- JUDI SHUFELT BEST

Becoming Parents

When an adult gives birth to her first child, she also gives birth to a parent.

- CAROL ORSBORN

Birth is the first experience of parenting. It may be the first time that you realize that all you can do is your best — but that you really can't take full responsibility for the outcome.

- LUCY SCOTT

It was life that would give her everything of consequence, life would shape her, not we. All we were good for was to make the introductions.

- HELEN HAYES

Taking care of a newborn baby means devoting yourself, body and soul, twenty-four hours a day, seven days a week, to the welfare of someone whose major response, in the way of positive reinforcement, is to throw up on you.

- DAVE BARRY

When newly born, a baby cries at the slightest frustration because up until now all its needs have been completely met. . . . It has never been cold, hungry or lonely.

- ELIZABETH DAVIS

People tell you how tired you'll be, but they don't tell you . . . that you'll be able to survive without much sleep because the simple act of looking at your baby is stirring, gratifying, energizing.

- CAROL WESTON

I remember leaving the hospital . . . thinking, 'Wait, are they going to let me just walk off with him? I don't know beans about babies!'

- ANNE TYLER

Bonding

A baby is something you carry inside you for nine months, in your arms for three years and in your heart till the day you die.

- MARY MASON

In the sheltered simplicity of the first days after a baby is born, one sees again the magical closed circle. The miraculous sense of two people existing only for each other.

- ANNE MORROW LINDBERGH

I saw his eyes open full to mine, and realized each of us was fastened to the other, not only by mouth and breast, but through our mutual gaze: the depth, calm, passion, of that dark blue, maturely focused look.

- ADRIENNE RICH

Perhaps the mother's attachment to her child is the strongest bond in the human. . . . The power of this attachment is so great that it enables the mother or father to make the unusual sacrifices necessary for the care of their infant day after day, night after night.

- MARSHALL KLAUS & JOHN KENNELL

Bonding *is* instinctive, but it is not instant and automatic.

- T. BERRY BRAZELTON

It is fortunate for their survival that babies are so designed by nature that they beguile and enslave mothers.

- JOHN BOWLBY

I held her for the first time and kissed her, and she went still and quiet as though by instinctive guile, and I was utterly enslaved by her flattery of my powers.

- LAURIE LEE

Our new baby has done his job well, the job all babies are
assigned: he has broken open my heart.

- DEBORAH KEENAN

This original mother-infant bond is the wellspring for all
the infant's subsequent attachments and is the formative
relationship in the course of which the child develops a
sense of himself.

- MARSHALL KLAUS & JOHN KENNELL

The precursor of the mirror is the mother's face.

- D.W. WINNICOTT

There is an amazed curiosity in every young mother. It is
strangely miraculous to see and to hold a living being
formed within oneself and issued forth from oneself.

- SIMONE de BEAUVOIR

The human baby should have the advantage of every
other newborn animal. He should seek his mother's
breast and feel his mothers' body as soon after birth as
possible and stay there. He should not be taken away to
cry alone in a nursery until someone comes along to give
routine care while his mother waits hungrily for him
down the hall.

- BARBARA GOLD as quoted by Morris Gold, M.D.

It is better that the mother discover her child by touching
it. . . . Better to feel before she sees. Better to sense this
warm and trembling life, to be moved in her heart by
what her *hands* tell her. To hold her child rather than
merely look at it.

- FREDERICK LeBOYER

Babies have delicate hands and lie with palms opened,
and you'd be astounded how much time a grown woman
can waste watching her infant rearrange his fingers.

- ANNA HEMPSTEAD BRANCH

New Mothers

The birth of a child is the greatest physical feat any person ever endures, an accomplishment deserving of at least a two-week rest. Instead, what follows are sleepless nights and interruptions all day long.

- LINDA LEWIS GRIFFITH

When the baby does come, he comes to stay. Twenty-four hours a day. Twenty-four hours a day for years and years and years. . . . You are never going to be without him again. When you get into this Mommy racket, you're in it for good.

- SHIRLEY JACKSON

When you are a mother, you are never really alone in your thoughts. You are connected to your child and to all those who touch your lives. A mother always has to think twice, once for herself and once for her child.

- SOPHIA LOREN

Motherhood has a very humanizing effect. Everything gets reduced to essentials.

- MERYL STREEP

After my daughter was born, I had to give some things up. You know, I don't really miss them.

- RITA AVERY

If you get help when the baby comes home, have the help do housework. *A mother should mother*.

- LEE SALK

If we don't take care of the mothers, they can't take care of their babies.

- JEANNE WATSON DRISCOLL

New Fathers

A new mother has been intimately acquainted with her baby for months before its birth, but a new *father* is suddenly introduced to a total stranger and is expected to demonstrate instantaneous love.

- JILINDA RICHER

To become a father is not hard, to be a father is, however.

- WILHELM BUSCH

A feeling of utter incompetence swept over me as he launched into . . . this world. . . . This little guy is a pretty fancy piece of equipment, but it didn't come with any instructions.

- TOM BODETT

There's plenty you can learn . . . from books, your friends and family, and your doctor . . . but the real training [in parenting] is on the job.

- BILL M. ATALLA

The magic intensity that is a part of this meeting is more than most men could ever imagine before they experience it. . . . After months of watching the woman he loves experience pregnancy, and a labor during which many of us feel frustratingly helpless, the sudden separate reality of the child is overwhelming.

- KEN DRUCK

I asked a friend with two small children for advice on getting ready for the baby. . . . He answered without hesitation, 'Just make sure your washing machine works and that you have a freezer full of food.'

- BILL M. ATALLA

The need to nurture is a natural masculine instinct.

- MARTIN GREENBERG

New parents quickly learn that raising children is a kind of desperate improvisation.

- BILL COSBY

Having a child, I discovered, makes you dream again and, at the same time, makes the dreams utterly real.

- CHARLES KRAUTHAMMER

A couple must come to grips with the fact that they have to stick together through this stressful time, or each will become lost in energy-sapping loneliness.

- SANDY JONES

A child is a grenade. When you have a baby, you set off an explosion in your marriage, and when the dust settles, your marriage is different from what it was. Not better, necessarily; not worse, necessarily; but different.

- NORA EPHRON

In trying to keep proving our love for (our) children, we ran the risk of ceasing to give to each other.

- PEARL BAILEY

Remember your husband? . . . He's the one your life revolved around. . . . You really were a team. . . . You liked it that way, and you vowed that having this baby wouldn't change what the two of you did. . . . But having young children puts a strain on the most secure marriage.

- LINDA LEWIS GRIFFITH

One of the ironies of having children is the way it confers adulthood and responsibility on you at the same time it makes you more dependent. Your children rely on you for meeting all their needs, while you become more dependent on each other.

- RANDY MEYERS WOLFSON & VIRGINIA DeLUCA

Meeting Baby's Needs

Like it or not, the very special little person in [your life] has special needs that must be met. Agreeing to meet those needs, rather than resisting them, brings parents into better harmony with their babies.

> - SANDY JONES

Adjusting your time so that your baby can feed when he is hungry may require self-discipline on your part, but you are presumed to be better than the baby at self-discipline.

> - CAROL BARTHOLOMEW

Responsive adults breed responsive babies, and . . . rigid disciplinarians of babies at this age breed spoiled, unhappy children with no confidence in themselves or their parents.

> - CHARLES & MARY ALDRICH

All healthy, normal infants do exactly what they can do and should be expected to do when they are ready. They should not be expected to do what they are not ready to do.

> - MAGDA GERBER

Nature vs. Nurture: Nature is beyond your control. Concentrate on nurture.

> - LESLIE LEHR SPIRSON

The baby whose cries are answered now will later be the child confident enough to show his independence and curiosity.

> - LEE SALK

Babies make people happy, [but] you have to make the baby happy first.

> - ANN OAKLEY

Responding to babies' needs is not the same as spoiling them. . . . This will result in contented babies, not little dictators. A contented baby is better equipped to handle the normal pains and frustrations that are part of being human than is a baby who is often frustrated and upset, but rarely comforted.
                    - MARY RENFREW, CHLOE FISHER & SUZANNE ARMS

Love is an essential part of the nourishment of every baby. . . . Unless he is loved, he will not grow and develop as a healthy organism — psychologically, spiritually, or physically.
                                        - ASHLEY MONTAGU

Mothers probably have soothed their babies by humming or singing to them since time immemorial. Many . . . adults have a non-verbal vocabulary of cooing and clucking nonsense sounds . . . only for communication with the very young.
                                        - RITA B. EISENBERG

The baby is practicing loving for life. The more he can love, now, and feel himself loved back, the more generous with . . . love he will be, right through his life.
                                        - PENELOPE LEACH

A baby learns he is loved through the simple, humdrum, over-and-over happenings of his life.
                                        - JAMES L. HYMES, Jr.

Spoil your baby. During the first year give him all the attention he wants, because this is when he is learning to love and trust. Later, . . . these feelings become the best basis for discipline.
                                        - LEE SALK

Breastfeeding

Breast feeding . . . provides a smooth transition from pregnancy to mutual independence. The baby has a close, loving start; his mother reaps innumerable benefits, many of which are so subtle that they cannot be described.

- LESTER DESSEZ HAZELL

It seemed ironic that we would have to convince professionals that breastfeeding was best, that God didn't make a mistake when He put human milk in breasts, and that we really are mammals.

- FREDERIC M. ETTNER

The closeness to the child resulting from breastfeeding is somehow an extension and affirmation of that very love that has resulted in its being there. . . . And this nurturing is to be treasured for its relationship that is to end all too soon, the very first of many partings.

- PRINCESS GRACE OF MONACO

Why a mother should nurse her child:
- It is the right milk for that particular baby.
- It never grows sour.
- You can carry it with you wherever you go.
- Since it's always the right temperature, it is
unnecessary to get up on a cold winter night to warm it.
- It comes in such cute containers.

- MARGARET GAMPER (from a medical student's paper)

I loved the look on my babies' faces when they had nursed their fill. The sheer relief and delight in their eyes and the smile of total satisfaction is language any mother can appreciate. It's proof that what you have to offer is the right stuff!

- INA MAY GASKIN

The survival of the human race has long depended on the satisfaction gained from the two voluntary acts of reproduction — intercourse and breastfeeding.
- NILES NEWTON

Learning to breast-feed from reading a book about it . . . is like learning to make love from reading a sex manual. Nursing, like good sex, takes lots of practice and a willing partner.
- ADRIENNE LIEBERMAN

The suckling relationship is one of the sources of real sweetness that we have in human existence. . . . The suckling baby can teach adults about the expression of sweet love and gratitude in a way that no words can.
- INA MAY GASKIN

Successful lactation is an expression of a woman's femininity and she doesn't need to count how often she feeds the baby any more than she counts how often she kisses the baby.
- BABETTE FRANCIS

One of the chief difficulties in viewing women's sexuality as a whole is that the taboos against some aspects of it are much greater than others. . . . The idea that successful breastfeeding gives sensuous pleasure is generally considered utterly unprintable.
- NILES NEWTON

Nursing remains an invaluable mothering tool to soothe hurts, calm an overtired and wound-up child, and create an island of safety in a sometimes unfriendly environment.
- KATHLEEN RANDOLPH

Nursing will provide you with an almost foolproof
excuse for not doing all sorts of tiresome things you
dislike and an equally legitimate reason for doing
pleasant things you enjoy.

- CAROL BARTHOLOMEW

Breastfeeding is a love relationship.

- SHEILA KITZINGER

All children eventually wean. We are very much afraid,
in our culture, to trust the child to grow, to progress, to
wean, to toilet-train, to eat, to sleep, to go to school in
due time at his or her own pace. We seem to constantly
feel that we must decide when it is best that the child do
these things.

- MARGARET NICHOLS

When my doctor learned my toddler was still nursing, he
asked, 'Do you think he'll still be interested in the breast
when he's eighteen?' My answer was: probably, but it
wouldn't be mine!

- THERESE NIESEN quoting a nursing mother

Forget about breast feeding if you really dislike the idea.
The chances are that no one thing—not breast feeding,
nor any one item of infant care—is going to make a
decisive difference to your child. It is the experience of
his whole early life, added up and taken together, which
produces the happy, healthy child.

- NILES NEWTON

Crying Babies

A human being who cries usually needs something, and a baby is no exception. . . . That something is usually to be held and nursed by a mother who is confident that this is her best role when her baby is little.

- LESTER DESSEZ HAZELL

Listening to a baby cry is a miserable occupation. Holding and soothing a baby is warm and happy.

- CAROL BARTHOLOMEW

Your baby's cry is a powerful distress signal, designed by nature so you won't ignore it.

- SANDY JONES

Letting a baby cry it out is a short-term solution whose long-term ramifications are not in the best interest of either baby or parents.

- MARIAN TOMPSON

Crying is as good for the lungs as bleeding is for the veins.

- LEE SALK, HERBERT RATNER, and others

There's no such thing as maternal instinct. You just try everything until something works.

- BEVERLY SLAPIN on the treatment of colic

A healthy child can scream for an incredibly long time.

- DAVID HASLAM

A mother or father picking up a crying baby lets him know that he has power in his universe and that he can do something to relieve his stress. This allows the baby to feel that he is not helpless and alone.

- CAROLE McKELVEY

If parents pick a crying baby up they needn't be afraid they are teaching him to control them. They are teaching him that something out there responds to the need he feels within.

- LEE SALK

The term 'difficult baby' reflects cultural expectations of what a baby *should be* and how a baby *should act*.

- LINDA M. CAPLAN

A mother's perception of her baby as 'bad' can become a self-fulfilling prophecy.

- SANDY JONES

All babies are good; some are just a little easier to live with than others.

- WILLIAM SEARS

Infants who are carried more cry less.

- RONALD G. BARR

Baby-wearing helps busy parents get to know their babies intimately.

- WILLIAM SEARS

To hell with housework. It takes all of your energy, mental as well as physical, to help the poor thing through the night.

- MOTHER OF A COLICKY BABY

When a child cries at night, most husbands appear to become suddenly stone-deaf. . . . When our children cried at night, [my wife] found my hearing could be toned up with the aid of a sharp kick!

- CHRISTOPHER GREEN

Babies & Sleep

We expect a great deal of a newborn baby when we
banish him to a separate, silent room all on his own after
he has spent nine months in the warmth and security of
his mother's womb.

- JANE ASHER

Before your baby was born, he was sleeping with you
every night, gently being held by your body and listening
to your breathing.

- DEBORAH BOEHLE

Whether it be on a Japanese 'futon,' or under an arctic
caribou skin, on the bare African ground, in a large four-
poster bed, or in double-twin size bed, whether they be
poor or rich, large or small, families all over the world
sleep together, and have done so since the beginning of
mankind.

- TINE THEVENIN

A baby needs its mother . . . even more in the dark than
in the daylight. In the dark the baby's predominant sense
— sight — is at rest. Instead, the baby needs to use its
sense of touch through skin-to-skin contact, and its sense
of smell.

- MICHEL ODENT, M. D.

The baby needs peace more than sleep. Believe it or not,
so do you. So don't struggle over sleep; just learn to be
peaceful together.

- POLLY BERRIEN BERENDS

An open door policy to the family bed is an integral part
of open communication and listening to the child's need. .
. . *The family bed* is a concept, part of a total picture, one
step toward rearing happy children.

- TINE THEVENIN

It's a lovely feeling to have a warm snuggly baby next to you in the bed to cuddle.

- JANE ASHER

Instead of the baby crying from a crib down the hall, he wakes up in the family bed with a beatific smile and can snack at the milk bar whenever he chooses. Mothers who sleep with their babies are meeting the child's fundamental needs for food, security, touch, and love.

- ELIZABETH NOBLE

It seems that nature meant for babies to stay in bed with Mother to insure a good night's sleep for both.

- PATRICIA SAVAGE

Sleep problems occur when your child's night-waking exceeds your ability to cope.

- WILLIAM SEARS

The first art of being a parent consists of sleeping when the baby isn't looking.

- OLD SAYING

The reason I'm so tired and you're not is that you get up when you want to and I get up when you want to.

- BEVERLY SLAPIN

In point of fact, we are all born rude. No infant has ever appeared yet with the grace to understand how inconsiderate it is to disturb others in the middle of the night.

- JUDITH MARTIN

Every morning I woke up tired and angry until I realized that sleep, as I knew it, no longer existed. Now, I only wake up tired.

- NANCY ISON

Accepting that we might not get a full night's sleep for a while is in itself a stress reliever.

- MARIAN TOMPSON

You can't teach your baby to sleep through the night. . . . But when the time is right, your baby's inborn master clock will set all of his internal operations in harmonious cycles, and his day and night rhythms will become more predictable.

- SANDY JONES

If you resent the interruptions to your sleep . . . you'll face each day more frustrated and try harder and harder to fit the baby into your sleep pattern. On the other hand, if you can adjust your mental aattitude to one of greater acceptance, you will find yourself able to enjoy those quiet moments in the night with your infant who needs to be held and nursed, or with your toddler who just needs to be with someone.

- PAT YEARIAN

I often feel a spiritual communion with all the other mothers who are feeding their babies in the still of the night. Having a baby makes me feel a general closeness with humanity.

- SIMONE BLOOM

I actually remember feelling delight, at two o'clock in the morning, when the baby woke for his feed, because I longed to have another look at him.

- MARGARET DRABBLE

Being a mom is definitely a drag when it comes to sleep. But, then again, when else do you get to be a guardian angel.

- LESLIE LEHR SPIRSON

Mother's Needs

During a pregnancy . . . it is relatively easy to get time and attention for yourself . . . . It is upsetting to find that hardly anyone shows care and tenderness to an exhausted mother struggling with a young baby.

- PADDY O'BRIEN

If you appear to be going through each day giving, giving, giving . . . well, you *are!* Being a wife and mother requires an open heart and great fortitude, but to be needed to such a degree brings its own rewards.

- ADELE BIRKBECK

Taking care of your own needs is no easy task when you feel responsible for the needs of your family.

- HAROLD BLOOMFIELD & LEONARD FELDER

Kids' needs are best met by parents whose needs are met.

- JEAN ILLSLEY CLARKE

It is usually up to Momma herself to see to her own needs, and to teach others how they can make her happy.

- ESTHER SCHIEDEL

We all need unconditional support, tenderness, cuddling, time and attention, some of the time. . . . When you are a mother, you do not stop needing some mothering.

- PADDY O'BRIEN

What I kept saying those first months was . . . 'I just haven't got it!' My husband kept asking me what 'it' was and I couldn't tell him. Then my mother decided to come for a visit. . . . When she hugged and kissed me, I turned to my husband and said, 'This is what *it* was!' I needed some mothering myself.

- EDA LESHAN quoting a new mother

Regardless of our age, we all have the desire at some time to feel babied and murtured by another, a pull to return to the conditions of infancy . . . . We need to recapture the sensations of being taken care of and protected by someone else, of not needing to do for ourselves.

- HELEN COLTON

Martyrs make poor parents!

- MARIANNE NEIFERT

There should be time in the day for a new mother to lie in a warm bath with lovely bath oil or bubbles, to feel cherished by the water.

- SHEILA KITZINGER

All I want is to finish a cup of coffee in the morning, . . . think a few thoughts, and take a shower when I want to. Is that too ambitious?

- BEVERLY SLAPIN

Some people dream of going to Hawaii to get away from it all. I just hope that some day I'll have privacy in the bathroom.

- SHIRLEY RADL

Beyond coping, I try to plan a genuine pleasure for every day—a visit with a friend, a concert or a play, an almond croissant instead of toast for breakfast or a bubble bath at the end of the day.

- ELIZABETH HORMANN

I could cope with my family very well if only I could take them by appointment.

- PHYLLIS NAYLOR

Fond as we are of our loved ones, there comes at times during their absence an unexplained peace.

- ANNE SHAW

We need time to dream, time to remember, and time to reach the infinite. Time to be.

- GLADYS TABER

So look for peace, love, beauty, order, harmony uncondi-tionally. Find them in the baby and in yourself. Enjoy being together. Together enjoy being.

- POLLY BERRIEN BERENDS

Why is it that to rise gladly at 4:00 am to meditate and meet one's God is considered a religious experience, and yet to rise at 4:00 am to serve the needs of one's helpless child is considered the ultimate in deprivation?

- PEGGY O'MARA

Mothering invites the habit of prayer for prayer is a natural builder of self-confidence. . . . Prayer is a great relaxation technique.

- MURSHIDA VERA JUSTIN CORDA

Meditation is really just quieting yourself enough so you can get in touch with your own inner wisdom.

- LOUISE HAY

One can learn sitting meditation by rocking and nursing a little one to sleep; one can learn reclining meditation by staying still to avoid disturbing a little one who has been awake for hours; and one can learn walking meditation by walking and swaying with a little one who would like to be asleep for hours. One *must* learn to breathe deeply in a relaxed and meditative manner in order to still the mind that doubts one's strength to go on, that sees every speck of dust on the floor and wants to clean it, and that tempts one to be up and about the busyness of accomplishments.

- PEGGY O'MARA

Parenthood
Parenting Is . . .

What good parenting gives our children is a running start in life, not lifelong immunity from difficulties.

- ELIZABETH HORMANN

Parenthood works in two directions: Good parenting makes for happy children; but it also makes for happy, fulfilled parents. It is not possible to give happiness without receiving it.

- DAVID STEWART

[The] most important principle for raising happy, well-adjusted, and mentally healthy children is to enjoy them.

- KATHARINE KERSEY

Too often, engrossed in the intense concentration necessary for making the 'right' decision, we miss out on much of the poetry, the music, and *joie de vivre* that is also part of being a parent.

- MARIAN TOMPSON

You have the right to make mistakes in bringing up your own children: blunder bravely! But believe more bravely that, on the whole, you are doing a good job of raising your children.

- FITZHUGH DODSON

Babies don't need . . . angels to raise them, nor paragons. . . . People will do. Ordinary people are all a baby asks for.

- JAMES L. HYMES, Jr.

Are anybody's parents typical?

- MADELEINE L'ENGLE

Nothing will ever be simple again, you think. Exciting, moving, tedious, frightening, wonderful, despairing, and all sorts of other feelings; but never simple. You are probably right.

- PADDY O'BRIEN

There is nothing more thrilling in this world, I think, than having a child that is yours, and yet is mysteriously a stranger.

- AGATHA CHRISTIE

What feeling is so nice as a child's hand in yours? So small, so soft and warm, like a kitten huddling in the shelter of your clasp.

- MARJORIE HOLMES

I am sure that if people had to choose between living where the noise of children never stopped and where it was never heard, all the good-natured and sound people would prefer the incessant noise to the incessant silence.

- GEORGE BERNARD SHAW

Families with babies and families without babies are sorry for each other.

- E. W. HOWE

Part of the good part of being a parent is a constant sense of *déjà vu*. But some of what you have to *vu* you never want to *vu* again.

- ANNA QUINDLEN

Parents are not really interested in justice, they just want quiet.

- BILL COSBY

The two things children wear out are clothes and parents.
- OLD SAYING

The Growing Parent

Who of us is mature enough for offspring before the offspring themselves arrive? The value of marriage is not that adults produce children but that children produce adults.

- PETER DeVRIES

Most of us become parents long before we have stopped being children.

- MIGNON McLAUGHLIN

Despite the increasing complexity of the task, parenthood remains the greatest single preserve of the amateur.

- ALVIN TOFFLER

There is something about having a baby that is wondrous: and then to raise that child into healthy adulthood—what a challenge.

- BARBARA WALTERS

When you become a parent it is your biggest chance to grow again. You have another crack at yourself.

- FRED ROGERS, 'Mister Rogers'

I believe our children, unknowingly and with innocent trickery, teach us the deeper knowledge of how to be a true human being.

- VIMALA McCLURE

In the effort to give good and comforting answers to the young questioners whom we love, we very often arrive at good and comforting answers for ourselves.

- RUTH GOODE

Dear God, I pray for patience. And I want it *right now!*

- OREN ARNOLD

We learn many things from children. Patience, for
instance.
                                    - FRANKLIN P. JONES

What signifies your Patience, if you can't find it when you
want it.
                                    - BENJAMIN FRANKLIN

No thing great is created suddenly, any more than a
bunch of grapes or a fig. If you tell me that you desire a
fig, I answer you that there must be time. Let it first
blossom, then bear fruit, then ripen.
                                    - EPICTETUS (first century A.D.)

The parents exist to teach the child, but also they must
learn what the child has to teach them; and the child has
a very great deal to teach them.
                                    - ARNOLD BENNETT

Growing up . . . that's what being a child is all about and
that's what being a parent is all about.
                                    - ANGELA BARRON Mc BRIDE

What you have become is the price you paid to get what
you used to want.
                                    - MIGNON McLAUGHLIN

A child strips away our illusions that we are perfect, that
we have it all figured out, that we are all grown up. In
fact, we grow up with our children if we are willing to
remain open to their innate goodness as well as our own.
                                    - PEGGY O'MARA

You will never really know what kind of parent you were
or if you did it right or wrong. Never. And you will
worry about this and them as long as you live. But when
your children have children and you watch them do what
they do, you will have part of an answer.
                                    - ROBERT FULGHUM

Guilt & Regret

Picture the wagon train finally arriving at Oregon Territory. Two mothers are walking alongside the wagon. One says, with self-criticism in her voice, 'I should have done more sewing along the way.'

'But when, Harriet? When could you have possibly done more sewing?'

'There was time, there was time. Between the Indian raid and the diphtheria epidemic.'

- JUDY SANDERS

Guilt: the gift that keeps on giving.

- ERMA BOMBECK

Guilt is not useful in *any* situation but *regret* is one of the most essential of all human attributes. . . . How about regretting what you did, forgiving yourself for your human frailty, and deciding what you would like to do about the situation?

- EDA LeSHAN

It's hard to fight an enemy who has outposts in your head.

- SALLY KEMPTON

Supermoms and superdads exist only on bumperstickers.
- DORIS JASINEK & PAMELA BELL RYAN

It is very easy to forgive others their mistakes. It takes more gut and gumption to forgive them for having witnessed your own.

- JESSAMYN WEST

If you haven't forgiven yourself something, how can you forgive others?

- DOLORES HUERTA

Motherhood

There's a lot more to being a woman than being a mother, but there's a hell of a lot more to being a mother than most people suspect.

- ROSEANNE BARR

The plain truth is that being a mother is the most important, difficult, and demanding of careers! At stake is the very life of another human being — and almost total responsibility for the life during its formative years.

- SHIRLEY RADL

Being a mother enables one to influence the future.

- JANE SELLMAN

To be a good mother a woman must have sense, and that independence of mind which few women possess who are taught to depend entirely on their husbands. Meek wives are . . . foolish mothers.

- MARY WOLLSTONECRAFT (19th century)

The commonest fallacy among women is that simply having children makes one a mother — which is as absurd as believing that having a piano makes one a musician.

- SYDNEY J. HARRIS

Women learn to like themselves in the mothering roles, which allow them experiences of love and power not easily found in other situations.

- LINDA GORDON

Motherhood is not a separate, pastel wing of emotion; it is a relationship as tricky and passionate as any other kind of love.

- MARNI JACKSON

A woman without a child may have a house that shines
but a woman with a child has a face that shines.
- INDIAN PROVERB

Motherhood is, in fact, never really learned. It evolves.
- SHEILA KITZINGER

Motherhood means being instantly interruptable,
responsive, responsible.
- TILLIE OLSEN

If you *don't* have a sense of humor — then hurry and
order one from your nearest catalog outlet. Motherhood
is no place to be without it.
- KENDRA LYNN MOTT

Motherhood brings as much joy as ever, but it still brings
boredom, exhaustion, and sorrow too. Nothing else ever
will make you as happy or as sad, as proud or as tired,
for nothing is quite as hard as helping a person develop
his own individuality — especially while you struggle to
keep your own.
- MARGUERITE KELLY & ELIA PARSONS

What is the price of an afternoon when a small girl is
soothed in your arms, when the sun bolts through a
doorway, and both you and the child are very young?
- DOROTHY EVSLIN

Motherhood is like Albania — you can't trust the
brochures — you have to go there.
- MARNI JACKSON

Some are kissing mothers and some are scolding
mothers, but it is love just the same, and most mothers
kiss and scold together.
- PEARL S. BUCK

Fatherhood

Men can and do make good mothers, but not many choose to go that route.

- MARNI JACKSON

It is not sexist to recognize the important differences between men and women and the different ways we each nurture.

- ROBERT MARK ALTER

Fatherhood is the only profession where you're guaranteed that the more effort you put into it the more enjoyment you will get out of it.

- WILLIAM SEARS

Fathers have a special excitement about them that babies find intriguing. . . . Fathers embody a delicious mixture of familiarity and novelty.

- LOUISE KAPLAN

It doesn't matter who my father was; it matters who I remember he was.

- ANNE SEXTON

The most important thing a father can do for his children is to love their mother.

- THEODORE HESBURGH

We modern, sensitive husbands realize that it's very unfair to place the entire child-care burden on our wives, so many of us are starting to assume maybe three percent of it.

- DAVE BARRY

Like any father, I have moments when I wonder whether I belong to my children or they belong to me.

- BOB HOPE

Parenting Ourselves

When we raise our children, we relive our childhood. . . .
When . . . we see or hear ourselves through [our
children's] eyes and ears, we meet the ghosts of our own
young parents.

- RICHARD LOUV

In becoming parents ourselves, we now understand what
our mother and father went through and thus can no
longer blame and denounce them.

- JUDITH VIORST

Perhaps our generation, in an effort to avoid making
'those same old mistakes,' has idealized parenting
beyond the scope of human achievement. . . . Allowing
our children to be *imperfect* requires more time, more
love.

- ROBIN LIM

Your parents . . . could not teach you anything that they
did not know. If your parents did not love themselves,
there was no way that they could teach you how to love
yourself.

- LOUISE HAY

If we have not been well loved as children, we must work
on our concepts of self-worth and self-love in adulthood
and take every opportunity to grow in appreciation of
ourselves.

- PEGGY O'MARA

Whether our parents loved us or whether they didn't is
no longer the question. Now the issue is — do we love
ourselves and do we accept love from everyone who is
willing to give it?

- JEAN ILLSLEY CLARKE

Children bring to us . . . this power of seeing the world as a new thing, as pure intuition, and so renewing for us the freshness of all life.

- JOYCE CAREY

Children can't be a center of life and a reason for being. They can be a thousand things that are delightful, interesting, satisfying, but they can't be a wellspring to live from.

- DORIS LESSING

But the hearts of small children are delicate organs. A cruel beginning in this world can twist them into curious shapes.

- CARSON McCULLERS

I was realizing that babies brought more amplification than change; I wasn't really different as much as more of myself.

- ROBERTA ISRAELOFF

Children recognize true feelings and can respond accordingly, love begets love, respect begets respect. Put out the effort and the rewards will arrive, with time, patience, and conviction.

- SKIP BERRY

Our children give us the opportunity to become the parents we always wished we'd had.

- LOUISE HART

Like every parent, I want nothing so much as my children's well-being. I want it so badly I may actually succeed in turning myself into a contented and well-adjusted person, if only for my children's sake.

- JOYCE MAYNARD

The Art of Parenting

It's practically universal for parents-to-be to express their determination to be 'perfect parents.' . . . They tell themselves they'll remember the mistakes their parents made and will never, ever make them.

- BILL M. ATALLA

I looked on child rearing not only as a work of love and duty but as a profession that was fully as interesting and challenging as any honorable profession in the world and one that demanded the best that I could bring to it.

- ROSE FITZGERALD KENNEDY

When you have a baby, your own creative training begins. Because of your child, you are now finding new powers and performing amazing feats.

- ELAINE MARTIN

Being a mother . . . is a constantly evolving process of adapting to the needs of your child while also changing and growing as a person in your own right.

- DEBORAH INSEL

A wise mother learns each day from quiet listening. Her parenting springs from her children's changing needs.

- VIMALA McCLURE

Trust your hunches. They're usually based on facts filed away just below the conscious level.

- JOYCE BROTHERS

The hardest part of raising children is teaching them to ride bicycles. . . . A shaky child on a bicycle for the first time needs both support and freedom. The realization that this is what the child will always need can hit hard.

- SLOAN WILSON

A mother understands what a child does not say.

> - JEWISH PROVERB

The quickest way for a mother to get her child's attention is to pick up the phone.

> - WILLOW NEWTON REED

Almost, the hardest of all is learning to be a well of affection, and not a fountain, to show them that we love them, not when *we* feel like it, but when they do.

> - NAN FAIRBROTHER

Praise them for important things, even if you have to stretch them a bit. Praise them a lot. They live on it like bread and butter and they need it more than bread and butter.

> - LAVINA CHRISTENSEN FUGAL

Try to see your children as whole and complete . . . as though they are already what they can become.

> - WAYNE DYER

A wise mother knows: There is no good child and no bad child. There is only *this* child.

> - VIMALA McCLURE

In this age of super-technology and with our fascination for . . . computers it is extremely difficult to face the fact that when we deal with children there are simply no . . . fool-proof techniques — and no magic.

> - EDA LESHAN

To use a computer analogy, each child is born with its own individual hardware. It is up to the parents to figure out (without a manual) which software works for that child. You will not have good results trying to raise a Macintosh child using IBM programs.

> - MORRIS MOEN

The Expanding Family

There is just *no* convenient time for having a baby. Every baby requires some change in the plans and way of living of the rest of the family. . . . even the sixth or seventh cause some changes.

- NILES NEWTON

If you want a baby, have a new one. Don't baby the old one.

- JESSAMYN WEST

This time I knew about the pain of childbirth. But I also knew about the joy of children. The motherhood mosaic has pieces that are dark and dull, but it's a work that shines.

- CAROL WESTON

The first child got me shiny new, like a new pair of shoes, but he got the blisters, too. The second child got me worn, yes, but comfortable.

- ANNA QUINDLEN

Comparison is a death knell to sibling harmony.

- ELIZABETH FISHEL

I got more children than I can rightly take care of, but I ain't got more than I can love.

- OSSIE GUFFY

Our third child changed our lives dramatically. It was the first time we were outnumbered.

- TOM & LESLIE McCLURE

It goes without saying that you should never have more children than you have car windows.

- ERMA BOMBECK

Civility & Discipline

The baby should be addressed in its own language. The language that precedes words. . . . We must go back still further and rediscover the universal language, which is simply the language of love.

- FREDERICK LeBOYER

The baby who has had a secure and cherished infancy is not going to be damaged by the discovery that there are limits set on his behavior. . . . Eventually he has to realize that in return for the considerate treatment he is given, he is expected to show consideration for others.

- CAROL BARTHOLOMEW

Guiding our children — lovingly — is an important part of caring for them and helping them be loving and lovable to people within our families and beyond.

- ELIZABETH HORMANN

Manners are a sensitive awareness of the feelings of others. If you have that awareness, you have good manners, no matter what fork you use.

- EMILY POST

If you want to be listened to, you should put in time listening.

- MARGE PIERCY

Civilization is just a slow process of learning to be kind.
- CHARLES L. LUCAS

We would like to think that children learn the civilizing virtues — caring, compassion, consideration — simply by our good example, but most children need a little more than that.

- ELIZABETH HORMANN

With discipline the only place to start is at the beginning. First we must help a child to live with himself and like himself, or he will never learn to adapt to or enjoy others.
- CAROL BARTHOLOMEW

Making a child feel loved is the first and most important part of good discipline.
- ROSS CAMPBELL

[Our] children need love, especially when they don't deserve it.
- HAROLD S. HULBERT

Discipline is not something you do *to* a child. It is something you do *with* a child.
- WILLIAM & MARTHA SEARS

We need to give children reasons for *behaving*, not reasons for *not misbehaving*!
- KATHARINE KERSEY

Children will work for attention from others, especially parents. . . . If they do not receive positive attention, then they will strive for negative attention since that is better than none at all.
- CAROLYN WEBSTER-STRATTON

An ounce of distraction is still worth a pound of exhortation.
- LA LECHE LEAGUE

Discipline comes from the same root as disciple, which means 'pupil' or 'learner.' It suggests that our function as parents is to guide or teach rather than judge.
- LOUISE HART

Discipline itself must be disciplined.
- M. SCOTT PECK

Wise is the mother who lets her child grow, explore, and develop, but yet can say 'No!'
- JEAN M. KAHLER

When you are in control, the children are much easier to keep under control. But when you are upset for any reason, the children are usually 'off the wall.' Children are sensitive; they respond dramatically to the emotional pulse of the mother.
- PAT HOLT & GRACE KETTERMAN

Discipline is the slow, bit by bit, time-consuming task of helping children to see the sense of acting in a certain way.
- JAMES L. HYMES, Jr.

If children are to learn to give up an absolute insistance on having their own way, so must their mothers.
- ELAINE HEFFNER

Pre-schoolers are still very little people. Their abilities to reason are undeveloped, and they will only be able to act and think in ways that are appropriate for their ages.
- LINDA LEWIS GRIFFITH

Parents have rarely said to a child, 'You're not bad, you're just young.'
- EDA LeSHAN

Being young is a fault which diminishes daily.
- SWEDISH PROVERB

Nothing is so strong as gentleness, nothing as gentle as true strength.
- St. FRANCIS de SALES

Govern a family as you would cook small fish — very gently.
- CHINESE PROVERB

Communication

Once a human being has arrived on this earth,
communication is the largest single factor determining
what kinds of relationships he makes with others and
what happens to him in the world about him.
- VIRGINIA SATIR

Communication is a process that works best between
equals who are concerned and care about each other.
- DON DINKMEYER

Teaching our children how to talk about frustration and
anger is one of our most important jobs as parents, and,
often, the larger part of that task is to teach ourselves
how to listen.
- HELEN NEVILLE AND MONA HALABY

Learning to be healthy parents sometimes means not
reacting and being willing to ask questions instead.
- BRIGID O'HARA CHASE

If you want something really exotic in the way of a
conversation with a child, ask a philosophical question.
-BARBARA WALTERS

You cannot truly listen to anyone and do anything else at
the same time.
- M. SCOTT PECK

We have two ears and only one tongue in order that we
may hear more and speak less.
- DIOGENES LAERTIUS (about 150 B.C.)

We cannot learn from one another until we stop shouting
at one another — until we speak quietly enough so that
our words can be heard as well as our voices.
- RICHARD M. NIXON

There are times when silence has the loudest voice.
- LEROY BROWNLOW

For children is there any happiness which is not also noise?
- FREDERICK W. FABER

To understand people, I must try to hear what they are *not* saying, what they perhaps will never be able to say.
- JOHN POWELL

A voice is a gift; it should be cherished and used to utter fully human speech if possible. Powerlessness and silence go together.
- MARGARET ATWOOD

When dealing with people, remember you are not dealing with creatures of logic, but with creatures of emotion.
- DALE CARNEGIE

Laughter is the shortest distance between two people.
-VICTOR BORGE

One can never speak enough of the virtues, the danger, the power of shared laughter.
- FRANÇOISE SAGAN

Trouble is a part of your life, and if you don't share it, you don't give the person who loves you enough chance to love you enough.
- DINAH SHORE

'Unbosom yourself,' said Wimsey. 'Trouble shared is trouble halved.'
- DOROTHY L. SAYERS

Parenting Advice in Perspective

Parenting books have enduring popularity precisely because no one has yet come up with the answers.

- PEGGY FINSTON

The more alternatives you have, the more likely you are to find something that works for you.

- ELIZABETH CRARY

No book can give you a 'blueprint' for raising your child, because you, your family and your child are unique. Books, however, can give information and insight, which you can adapt to your own situation. Don't raise your child 'by the book' but 'by the child.'

- LYNN MOEN

As time passes we all get better at blazing a trail through the thicket of advice.

- MARGOT BENNETT

Advice is what we ask for when we already know the answer but wish we didn't.

- ERICA JONG

What good mothers and fathers instinctively feel like doing for their babies is the best after all.

- BENJAMIN SPOCK

The problem with books on discipline is that they never discuss the situations that come up at our house.

- PHYLLIS NAYLOR

The best thing to read when trying to raise a child is the child. Maybe it is even more important that we learn to read ourselves.

- POLLY BERRIEN BERENDS

Anything which parents have not learned from
experience they can now learn from their children.

-OLD SAYING

If you want to understand the needs of children, observe
and study the child.

-MARIA MONTESSORI

'Beware of the experts. Haven't you noticed that they
have all the answers—but they don't always agree?'
'So who's the expert? Me?' He smiled at me and shook
his head. He held his finger out and my daughter curled
her little hand around it. 'She is.'

- LESLIE LEHR SPIRSON & HER PEDIATRICIAN

Praise vs. Blame

The world will be a better and a happier place when
people are praised more and blamed less; when we utter
in their hearing the good we think and also gently
intimate the criticisms we hope may be of service.

- FRANCIS E. WILLARD

Words are more powerful than perhaps anyone suspects,
and once deeply engraved in a child's mind, they are not
easily eradicated.

- MAY SARTON

Any fool can criticize, condemn, and complain — and
most fools do.

- DALE CARNEGIE

He has the right to criticize who has the heart to help.

- ABRAHAM LINCOLN

To belittle is to be little.

- OLD SAYING

Self Esteem

If the baby's body is a joy and a delight in the mother's arms, that same body will become a joy and a delight to its owner later on.
                              - O. SPURGEON ENGLISH & GERALD H.J. PEARSON

When you make children feel guilty they compromise their integrity for your love.
                              - DORIS JASINEK & PAMELA BELL RYAN

How we accept our children has a profound impact on how they accept themselves.
                              - PEGGY FINSTON

The way a child is viewed by his parents — and the way he views himself — is crucial. View him as a promise rather than a problem or a project.
                              - POLLY BERRIEN BERENDS

How well a child responds to discipline depends primarily on how much the child feels loved and accepted. So our biggest task is to make him feel loved and accepted.
                              - ROSS CAMPBELL

By focusing on building self-esteem and self-confidence in our kids . . . [we] give them an armor they take with them wherever they go, through their childhood and adolescence and into adulthood. An internalized armor.
                              - RICHARD LOUV

Sometimes people confuse human 'being' with human 'doing' and they judge others by their accomplishments. When that happens to children, they feel they have to earn love. Unfortunately, those children become adults who never feel good about themselves — no matter how much they accomplish.
                              - STEPHEN GARBER & MARIANNE GARBER

The function of loving parents is not to try to make a child over but to help him discover what he is like and to like being that way.

- LYNN MOEN

Everybody is all right really.

- A. A. MILNE

Self-esteem is not a safety-deposit box, filled at one point in our life, locked, and there forever. Rather it is like a bucket of water with a hole in it (and some of us have larger holes in our bucket than others) that must continuously be refilled to stay at a healthy level when it's been leaking for awhile. Success in life's experiences lets us refill our own buckets with feelings of self-worth. But they also are refilled by the loving and caring words and actions of those around us.

- VICKI LANSKY

When we allow children to do for themselves and then laud their efforts, they develop competence and a readiness to tackle tasks ahead.

- DORIS JASINEK & PAMELA BELL RYAN

It is important to fail and important to give our children permission to fail.

- CAROLE HYATT & LINDA GOTTLEIB

Imperfection is God's gift. It makes us compassionate as well as deserving of compassion.

- ROBIN LIM

A lot of people are concerned about the losers and I am too. . . . [But I'm also] concerned about the winners because there is usually only one winner and that can be a very lonely position to be in.

- FRED ROGERS

Your children are not you. To try to show the world what
a good mother you are diminishes you. To try to show
the world what good children you have diminishes them.
- VIMALA McCLURE

A low self-love in the parent desires that his child should
repeat his character and fortune. . . . Cannot we let people
be themselves, and enjoy life in their own way? You are
trying to make another you. One's enough.
- RALPH WALDO EMERSON

How many cares one loses when one decides not to be
something, but to be someone.
- GABRIELLE 'COCO' CHANEL

High self-esteem is not a noisy conceit. It is a quiet sense of
self-respect, a feeling of self-worth. When you have it
deep inside, you're glad you're you.
- DOROTHY CORKILLE BRIGGS

No one can make you feel inferior without your consent.
- ELEANOR ROOSEVELT

With effort and a few basic changes, parents can enhance
their own self-esteem and that of every family member. . .
. For parents and children really want the same thing; to
be respected and be found both worthwhile and lovable.
- ELLEN SHAFER

Parents as Models

Train up a child in the way he should go: and when he is old, he will not depart from it.

- PROVERBS 22:6

Train up a child in a way he should go — and walk there yourself once in a while.

- JOSH BILLINGS

A good example is the best sermon.

- HERBERT J. TAYLOR

Children are, after all, our mirrors. They play back to us what they have learned from us.

- PEGGY O'MARA

Children are like wet cement. Whatever falls on them makes an impression.

- HAIM GINOTT

Children are unpredictable. You never know what inconsistency they're going to catch you in next.

- FRANKLIN P. JONES

Children are natural mimics — they act like their parents in spite of every attempt to teach them good manners.

- OLD SAYING

Do not *say* things. What you *are* stands over you the while, and thunders so I cannot hear what you say to the contrary.

- RALPH WALDO EMERSON

Kids learn more from example than anything you say. I'm convinced they learn very early not to hear anything you say, but watch what you do.

- JANE PAULEY

What a father says to his children is not heard by the world, but it will be heard by posterity.

- JEAN PAUL RICHTER

Children have never been very good at listening to their elders, but they have never failed to imitate them. They must, they have no other models.

- JAMES BALDWIN

Don't worry that your children never listen to you; worry that they are always watching you.

- ROBERT FULGHUM

Judicious mothers will always keep in mind that they are the first book read, and the last put aside, in every child's library.

- C. LENOX REDMOND

Children deserve parents who feel good about themselves.   - JEAN ILLSLEY CLARKE

Perhaps the greatest gift that women can give their daughters is to take precious care of their own lives — to develop their natural talents and to honor the opportunities that come their way. By so doing, they become vital models for their children as well as full women in their own right.

- EVELYN BASSOFF

It is difficult to give children a sense of security unless you have it yourself. If you have it, they catch it from you.

- WILLIAM C. MENNINGER

If you must hold yourself up to your children as an object lesson . . . hold yourself up as an example and not as a warning.

- GEORGE BERNARD SHAW

Childhood
Children Are . . .

Children come into the world endowed with new
energies that could correct the errors of past generations
and give a new breath of life to the world.

- MARIA MONTESSORI

The surface of a table can be cluttered and breakable in
exact proportion to the age of the children who pass it by.

- DOROTHY EVSLIN

Children are like jam: all very well in the proper place,
but you can't stand them all over the shop — eh, what?

- EDITH NESBIT

Even when freshly washed and relieved of all obvious
confections, children tend to be sticky.

- FRAN LEBOWITZ

There are only two things a child will share willingly —
communicable diseases and his mother's age.

- BENJAMIN SPOCK

That energy which makes a child hard to manage is the
energy which afterwards makes him a manager of life.

- HENRY WARD BEECHER

A two-year-old is probably one of the few creatures on
earth who could survive a shipwreck without the blink of
an eye and then become hysterical when her juice is
poured in the wrong cup.

- WANDA TAYLOR

Childhood is a place as well as a time.

- MAY SARTON

Remember what the three-to-fiver is about. She's trying to figure out the system, *not to beat it,* at first. . . .

A granddaughter came to visit. We called her from the swing for lunch. She went on swinging. We called her twice. She asked us to push her. We said, 'What's the matter, Laurie, don't you come to lunch at your house when lunch is ready?' Her answer, 'Yes, Grandma, Mommy calls me three times. Daddy calls me once. I wanted to see how many times you call.'

TESTING, TESTING, TESTING IS THE NAME OF THE GAME.

- STELLA CHESS & JANE WHITBREAD

The four-year-old is not an incomplete adult, but a complete and whole four-year-old. Childhood when lived fully prepares for adulthood perfectly.

- JOSEPH CHILTON PEARCE

The real menace in dealing with a five-year-old is that in no time at all you begin to sound like a five-year-old.

- JEAN KERR

It is not easy to be crafty and winsome at the same time, and few accomplish it after the age of six.

- F. GARDNER REESE

A child's spirit is like a child, you can never catch it by running after it; you must stand still, and for love, it will soon itself come back.

- ARTHUR MILLER

Childhood is frequently a solemn business for those inside it.

- GEORGE WILL

Allow a child the privilege of being a child.
He will be one for such a brief moment.

- JAMES DOBSON

Childhood, A Short Season

Our children are our most important guests, who enter
into our home, ask for careful attention, stay for awhile,
and then leave to follow their own way.

- HENRI NOUWEN

All children, except one, grow up.

- J.M. BARRIE

We are all so busy . . . that we seldom have time to . . .
savor where we are. Yet babies and young children have
no sense of the future. . . . They are creatures of the
moment.

- STELLA CHESS & JANE WHITBREAD

It's easy to complain about children. But when we want
to express our joy, our love, the words elude us. The
feelings are almost so sacred they defy speech.

- JOAN McINTOSH

Once the children were in the house the air became more
vivid and more heated; every object in the house grew
more alive.

- MARY GORDON

It will be gone before you know it. The fingerprints on
the wall appear higher and higher. Then suddenly they
disappear.

- DOROTHY EVSLIN

If you bungle raising your children, I don't think
whatever else you do well matters very much.

- JACQUELINE KENNEDY ONASSIS

Meeting Children's Needs

Children are not adults with little bodies. They have characteristics of their own, and we must respond to them as they are rather than as we would like them to be.
-EUGENE M. ANDERSON, CHARLOTTE ROGERS & GEORGE REDMAN

We need to find time to spend alone with our children. This means . . . being willing to say no to obligations that interfere with family togetherness, and making and keeping 'appointments' with family members — by making daily conscious choices to put family first.
- PEGGY O'MARA

The eighties notion of quality time misses the point. I advocate *quantity* time. Why? Because the real fun of being a parent, and the lasting bond between parent and child, can only be experienced over time — lots of time.
- BILL M. ATALLA

Your children need your presence more than they need your presents.
- JESSE JACKSON

Every child needs a lap.
- BENJAMIN WEININGER & HENRY RABIN

Children need you the most when they're at their worst. People need each other the most when they're at their worst.
- DORIS JASINEK & PAMELA BELL RYAN

What your child needs from you is mothering or fathering — not psychologizing.
- LEE SALK

Instant availability without continuous presence is probably the best role a mother can play.
- LOTTE BAILYN

[Your toddler] doesn't want interference from you, but he does depend on your being there for support and encouragement.

-ELAINE MARTIN

Children occasionally need the sort of benevolent neglect that allows a flower to choose its own time and place to blossom.

- SALLY JAMES

The fastest road to furthering independence in your children is total attention to the needs of your children in their dependent years.

- HERBERT RATNER

If you fully meet a child's needs when they first appear, the needs will go away. If you do not meet a child's needs when they appear, the needs will come back later in the child's life.

- WILLOW NEWTON REED

You can't force a child to be independent, you can only force him not to depend on *you*.

- PAT YEARIAN

If you make children happy now, you will make them happy twenty years hence by the memory of it.

- KATE DOUGLAS WIGGIN

Sleep

No day is so bad it can't be fixed with a nap.

- CARRIE SNOW

Small children disturb your sleep, big children your life.

- YIDDISH PROVERB

Anyone who thinks the art of conversation is dead ought to tell a child to go to bed.

- ROBERT GALLAGHER

There was never a child so lovely but his mother was glad to get him asleep.

- RALPH WALDO EMERSON

The best time for parents to put the children to bed is while they still have the strength.

- HOMER PHILLIPS

The peace which radiates from a sleeping child is . . . not quite of this world. But it can give something to . . . to parents, if our eyes and hearts are open to it.

- GUDRUN DAVY

After you've made your rounds you fall asleep in the center, watched over by your bear, your camel, your mobile. Watched over by me.

- PHYLLIS CHESLER

Seeing you sleeping peacefully . . . among your stuffed ducks, bears and basset hounds, . . . would remind me that no matter how good the next day might be, certain moments were gone forever.

- JOAN BAEZ

Families on the Go

A suburban mother's role is to deliver children
obstetrically once, and by car forever after.

- PETER DeVRIES

If a woman's place is in the HOME, why am I always in
the CAR?

- BUMPER STICKER

It seems to me I spent my life in car pools, but you know,
that's how I kept track of what was going on.

- BARBARA BUSH

I suppose there must be in every mother's life the
inevitable moment when she has to take two small
children shopping in one big store.

- SHIRLEY JACKSON

In America there are two classes of travel — first class,
and with children. Travelling with children corresponds
roughly to travelling third-class in Bulgaria. They tell me
there is nothing lower in the world than third-class
Bulgarian travel.

- ROBERT BENCHLEY

We wander for distraction, but we travel for fulfillment.

-HILAIRE BELLOC

Keep close to Nature's heart . . . and break clear away,
once in awhile, and climb a mountain or spend a week in
the woods. Wash your spirit clean.

-JOHN MUIR

[While traveling,] children behave best when their
stomachs are full and their bladders are empty.

- VICKI LANSKY

Food

A child is fed with milk and praise.

- MARY LAMB

A man finds out what is meant by spitting image when he tries to feed cereal to his infant.

- IMOGENE FRY

The decision to eat strained lamb or not to eat strained lamb should be with the 'feedee' not the 'feeder.' Blowing strained lamb into the feeder's face should be accepted as an opinion, not as a declaration of war.

- ERMA BOMBECK

It is easy to become so bogged down in the tedious necessity of getting enough eggs, fruit, vegetables, meat, and juice down Allan's throat that you lose sight of your larger aim, which is to get Allan to like good food and enjoy the process of eating it.

- CAROL BARTHOLOMEW

To drink milk will be the least absorbing activity in connection with the cup, while he is conducting research on the nature of the cup. He examines the outer surface of the cup, explores the inner surface, discovers its hollowness, bangs it on the tray for its sound effects. Rivers of milk, orange juice and water cascade from cup to tray to kitchen floor, adding joy to the experiment.

- SELMA FRAIBERG

Offerings of food have been breaking down barriers for centuries.

- ESTÉE LAUDER

We love those we feed, not vice versa; in caring for others we nourish our own self-esteem.

- JESSAMYN WEST

I'm not sure how many people consider packing a
lunchbox for their child to be an act of love, but I firmly
believe it is.

- MARLENE ANNE BUMGARNER

A great truth I have learned when preparing meals for
children: The more effort you put into it, the more you
resent them when they don't like it.

- TANIA WRIGHT

I was not a classic mother. But my kids were never
palmed off to boarding school. So, I didn't bake cookies.
You can buy cookies, but you can't buy love.

- RAQUEL WELCH

I'm not a cookie-baking mother. Well, that's not true. I am
a cookie-baking mother. I'm exactly a cookie-baking
mother, but I'm not a traditional cookie-baking mother.

- CHER

I always make the [birthday] cake. I feel like it puts me in
touch with the elemental aspects of motherhood: that is,
I get to lick the bowl.

- ANNA QUINDLEN

Traditions & Celebrations

Ritual is endless and beautiful. You can find it all around you. . . . It tells us who we are. We find our roots in ritual, in our ethnic background and in our ancestors.
- SARAH TAYLOR

Small traditions serve as beacons toward the future: twinkling stars in the present that can brighten our days.
- BETSY CARLSON

We create our own traditions for the same reason we create our own families. To know where we belong.
- ELLEN GOODMAN

By building traditions . . . that emphasize the importance of being a member of this family, we create a source of love and personal pride and belonging that makes living in a chaotic world easier.
- SUSAN LIEBERMAN

Family traditions give children a sense of identity and help them understand and appreciate their heritage.
- BETSY CARLSON

Family jokes, though rightly cursed by strangers, are the bond that keeps most families alive.
- STELLA BENSON

I want to . . . create celebrations which raise the daily and momentary to the universal and eternal; meal times, bedtimes, . . . weekends, holidays or the discovery of a lost thimble are all potential celebrations.
- MARGLI MATTHEWS

Memories of family traditions increase in value as the years go by.
- BETSY CARLSON

Play

Children's play should be regarded as their most serious actions.

-MICHEL de MONTAIGNE

Play helps a child find out who he is or where she fits in. In fact, play is a child's most important activity.

- DORIS JASINEK & PAMELA BELL RYAN

We may not be sure what kind of play children need at different times . . . but fortunately children have a way of letting us know.

- FRED ROGERS & BARRY HEAD

Nothing that human beings do, know, think, hope and fear that has not been attempted, experienced, practiced or at least anticipated in children's games.

- HEIDI BRITZ-CRECELIUS

You can't help but feel a little bit silly at the age of forty riding a merry-go-round or building a sand castle by yourself. Our kids give us an excuse to be kids again.

- JOHN BOSWELL & RON BARRETT

Your caring presence and a good sense of silliness are what is required of you in your baby's world.

- ELAINE MARTIN

How much easier it is to have two children under the age of four if you are not only able but willing to do lifelike monkey imitations.

- ANNA QUINDLEN

Spontaneity is the quality of being able to do something just because you feel like it at the moment, of trusting your instincts, of taking yourself by surprise.

- RICHARD IANNELLI

The child had every toy his father wanted.
- ROBERT E. WHITTEN

Feeling that you must have every toy, every device, every piece of equipment merely places objects between you and your child.
- VIMALA McCLURE

There are many ways to enlarge [your child's] world. Love of books is the best of all.
- JACQUELINE KENNEDY ONASSIS

Books are the quietest and most constant of friends; they are the most accessible and wisest of counsellors, and the most patient of teachers.
- CHARLES W. ELIOT

Reading a book over and over shares the familiar comfort of hot water bottles and thumbsucking.
- MARGARET ATWOOD

When you reread a classic you do not see more in the book than you did before; you see more in you than there was before.
- CLIFTON FADIMAN

The best books to buy for young children are those *you'll* enjoy reading aloud over and over and over again.
- LYNN MOEN

We shouldn't teach great books; we should teach a love of reading.
- B. F. SKINNER

Babies do not want to hear about babies; they like to be told of giants and castles, and of somewhat which can stretch and stimulate their little minds.
- SAMUEL JOHNSON

Imagination & Creativity

Of all people children are the most imaginative. They abandon themselves without reserve to every illusion.
- J. B. MacAULAY

The illusions of childhood are necessary experiences: a child should not be denied a balloon because an adult knows that sooner or later it will burst.
- MARCELENE COX

The richness of the child's imagination will depend on the wealth of experiences he has had, from infancy on.
- JAMES L. HYMES, Jr.

Only when I make room for the voice of the child within, do I feel myself to be genuine and creative.
- ALICE MILLER

The person who has no imagination has no wings.
- MUHAMMAD

Imagination is the highest kite that can fly.
- LAUREN BACALL

One can never consent to creep when one feels an impulse to soar.
- HELEN KELLER

Discovery consists of seeing what everybody has seen and thinking what nobody has thought.
- ALBERT SZENT-GYÖRGYI

A new idea is delicate. It can be killed by a sneer or a yawn; it can be stabbed to death by a quip and worried to death by a frown.
- CHARLES BROWER

If you go through life convinced that your way is always best, all the new ideas in the world will pass you by.
- AKIO MORITA

Practical people would be a lot more practical if they were just a little more dreamy.
- J. P. McEVOY

Imagination is rooted in reality.
- JAMES L. HYMES, Jr.

Imagination is the beginning of creation. You imagine what you desire, you will what you imagine, and at last you create what you will.
- GEORGE BERNARD SHAW

Without this playing with fantasy no creative work has ever yet come to birth. The debt we owe to the play of imagination is incalculable.
- CARL GUSTAV JUNG

The most beautiful thing we can experience is the mysterious. It is the source of all true art and science.
- ALBERT EINSTEIN

If you have built castles in the air, your work need not be lost; that is where they should be. Now put the foundations under them.
- HENRY DAVID THOREAU

As long as we think dugout canoes are the only possibility — all that is real or can be real — we will never see the ship, we will never feel the wind blow.
- SONIA JOHNSON

Exploring The World

Young children love the whole world. There is no awareness of danger to an exploring toddler, only an awareness of joyful discovery.

- JEAN ARMON

Any adult who spends even fifteen minutes with a child outdoors finds himself drawn back to his own childhood, like Alice falling down the rabbit hole.

- SHARON MacLATCHIE

Children, like animals, use all their senses to discover the world.

- EUDORA WELTY

I have always felt the more experiences a child has . . . the more interested in life he is likely to be.

- ROSE FITZGERALD KENNEDY

Let our children grow tall and some taller than others if they have it in them to do so.

- MARGARET THATCHER

Perhaps we have been misguided into taking too much responsibility from our children, leaving them too little room for discovery.

- HELEN HAYES

I love to think that the day you're born, you're given the world as a birthday present.

- LEO BUSCAGLIA

If I were given the opportunity to present a gift to the next generation, it would be the ability for each individual to learn to laugh at himself.

- CHARLES SCHULZ

If I had influence with the good fairy who is supposed to preside over the christening of all children I should ask that her gift to each child in the world would be a sense of wonder so indestructible that it would last throughout life as an unfailing antidote against the boredom and disenchantment of later years, the sterile preoccupation with things that are artificial, the alienation from the sources of our strength.

- RACHEL CARSON

I think, at a child's birth, if a mother could ask a fairy godmother to endow it with the most useful gift, that gift should be curiosity.

- ELEANOR ROOSEVELT

Adventure is worthwhile in itself.

- AMELIA EARHART

All our dreams can come true—if we have the courage to pursue them.

- WALT DISNEY

And I perpetually await a rebirth of wonder.

- LAWRENCE FERLINGHETTI

If a child is to keep alive his inborn sense of wonder without any such gift from the fairies, he needs the companionship of at least one adult who can share it, rediscovering with him the joy, excitement and mystery of the world we live in.

- RACHEL CARSON

Teaching & Learning

The whole art of teaching is only the art of awakening the natural curiosity of young minds for the purpose of satisfying it afterwards.

- ANATOLE FRANCE

I am not a teacher, but an awakener.

- ROBERT FROST

Education is not the filling of a pail, but the lighting of a fire.

- WILLIAM BUTLER YEATS

The central task of education is to implant a will and facility for learning; it should produce not learned but learning people. . . . In a time of drastic change it is the learners who inherit the future. The learned usually find themselves equipped to live in a world that no longer exists.

- ERIC HOFFER

Parents who fill the house with books, painting, and music, who have interesting friends and discussions, who are curious and ask questions, provide children with all the intellectual stimulation they need.

- DAVID ELKIND

A parent who talks happily with a small child — and listens seriously in return — is helping creativity to grow.

- JOAN BECK

Minor things can become moments of great revelation when encountered for the first time.

- MARGOT FONTEYN

Treat people as if they were what they ought to be, and you help them to become what they are capable of being.

- JOHANN WOLFGANG von GOETHE

Growth occurs in many small steps.

- ELIZABETH CRARY

You cannot teach a child to take care of himself unless you will let him try to take care of himself. He will make mistakes; and out of these mistakes will come his wisdom.

- FRANCIS BACON

The single most significant secret to all good education . . . is timing. The trick is to teach when someone is able to learn, and when he wants to be taught.

- JAMES L. HYMES, Jr.

When the mind is ready, a teacher appears.

- ZEN SAYING

Children require guidance and sympathy far more than instruction.

- ANNE SULLIVAN

You can't teach children to think by telling them what to do.

- ELIZABETH CRARY

Too often we give children answers to remember rather than problems to solve.

- ROGER LEVIN

Perhaps the most valuable result of all education is the ability to make yourself do the thing you have to do, when it ought to be done, whether you like it or not.
- THOMAS HENRY HUXLEY

Knowledge begets knowledge. The more I see, the more impressed I am — not with what we know — but with how tremendous the areas are that are as yet unexplored.
- JOHN GLENN

The right amount [of help] is the least help the child
needs in order to be successful.

- JAMES L. HYMES, Jr.

Do not handicap your children by making their lives
easy.

- ROBERT A. HEINLEIN

If you want to learn something well, then teach it.

- WALTER TROBISCH

Experience is a hard teacher because she gives the test
first, the lesson afterwards.

- VERN LAW

It is the true nature of mankind . . . to learn from
mistakes, not from example.

- SIR FRED HOYLE

I hear and I forget. I see and I remember. I do and I
understand.

- CHINESE PROVERB

Information's pretty thin stuff unless mixed with
experience.

- CLARENCE DAY

Paradoxically, what people most need to learn, they
cannot be *taught* or *educated* to do.

- IVAN ILLICH

Education consists mainly in what we have unlearned.

- MARK TWAIN

We cannot always build the future for our youth, but we
can build our youth for the future.

- FRANKLIN D. ROOSEVELT

Teens - Growth & Maturity

Between the ages of twelve and seventeen a parent can age thirty years.

- SAM LEVENSON

Now we seek direction, not permission.

- CYNTHIA ORANGE

The essential thing about mothers — one needs to know that they are there, particularly at that age when, paradoxically, one is trying so hard to break away.

- MARGOT FONTEYN

One of the oldest human needs is having someone to wonder where you are when you don't come home at night.

- MARGARET MEAD

Any kind of growth that's worth having causes struggle and pain.

- EDA LeSHAN

A boy becomes an adult three years before his parents think he does, and about two years after he thinks he does.

- LEWIS B. HERSHEY

When I was a boy of fourteen, my father was so ignorant I could hardly stand to have the old man around. But when I got to twenty-one, I was astonished at how much he had learned in seven years.

- MARK TWAIN

If we try to control and hold onto our children, we lose them. When we let them go, they have the option of returning to us more fully.

- ANNE WILSON SCHAEF

A teenager's job is to move away from you; to grow up, to be a unique, strong adult. Ours is to let it happen, as quickly or slowly as necessary, but thoroughly. If we labor in this way, we'll experience a birth; we'll have a very wonderful new adult friend, our own daughter or son.

- KAREN VALENTINE EDMAN

The best compliment to a child . . . is the feeling you give him that he has been set free to make his own inquiries, to come to conclusions that are right for him, whether or not they coincide with your own.

- ALISTAIR COOK

There are only two lasting bequests we can hope to give our children. One of these is roots; the other, wings.

- HODDING CARTER

When wings are grown, birds and children fly away.

- CHINESE PROVERB

Children are the power and the beauty of the future. Like tiny falcons we can release their hearts and minds, and send them soaring, gathering the air to their wings, searching for the knowledge it is their right to want.

- SKIP BERRY

Although giving in to the adolescent's unreasonable demand is a sign of parental weakness, negotiating with her toward an acceptable compromise is a sign that the family is healthy, growing, and changing.

- EVELYN BASSOFF

The trouble with teenagers is that half the time they want you to treat them like adults and half the time like children, and you always guess wrong.

- LaVANCE DAVIS

The trouble with trouble is that it starts out as fun.

- OLD SAYING

The trouble is that growing up is a full-time job.

- PEG BRACKEN

Parents should understand that the teenage years are a time when they have to step back and let their teenagers make their own mistakes. . . .The best thing a parent can do is listen, be there, and reserve judgement.

- JULIANA KORTE (as a teenager)

Parents should give a child more and more responsibility each year, so that when he gets beyond their control he will no longer need it.

- JAMES DOBSON

If you want your children to keep their feet on the ground, put some responsibility on their shoulders.

- ABIGAIL VAN BUREN

A mother is not a person to lean on but a person to make leaning unnecessary.

- DOROTHY CANFIELD FISHER

Here is the crux of the parenting experience — being there when you're needed, out of the way when you're not, and able to recognize the difference.

- PENNY COLMAN

Eventually I learned that some things matter while others don't. And I learned that if you harp on those that don't, you'll lose out on those that do. Being in school, for instance, matters. Three earrings in one ear don't . . . not really. Coming in on time matters. Fingernails painted black don't. A fairly even disposition, especially in a family where teen-agers are in the majority, matters. Alice Cooper posters on the bedroom wall don't.

- ANN COMBS

Respect

Respect the child. Be not too much his parent. Trespass not on his solitude.

- RALPH WALDO EMERSON

Respect: to look more at, to consider worthy of high regard, to show consideration or esteem. Respect is the basis of all good human relationships, particularly with our children.

- LYNN MOEN

Children are likely to live up to what you believe of them.

- LADY BIRD JOHNSON

Everyone old enough to have a secret is entitled to have some place to keep it.

- JUDITH MARTIN (Miss Manners)

The child who feels your respect during silences is nourished more than the child who is constantly fussed and chattered over.

- VIMALA McCLURE

We are not doing our children any favors by allowing them to 'get away' with disrespect, especially towards us.

- PEGGY FINSTON

When we are polite to children, we show in the most simple and direct way possible that we value them as people and care about their feelings.

- DAVID ELKIND

Just by speaking courteously, you may be able to bring out the very best in the people you live with. Give them a chance to talk. Listen patiently. And soften your voice.

- DORIS JASINEK & PAMELA BELL RYAN

Few parents nowadays pay any regard to what their children say to them. The old-fashioned respect for the young is fast dying out.

- OSCAR WILDE

Only if we become sensitive to the fine and subtle ways in which a child may suffer humiliation can we hope to develop the respect for him that a child needs.

- ALICE MILLER

He that will have his son respect his orders, must himself have a great respect for his son.

- JOHN LOCKE

From the moment they are born [our children have a] right to respect. We keep them children for too long, their world separate from the real world of life.

- PEARL S. BUCK

The sooner you treat your son as a man, the sooner he will be one.

- JOHN DRYDEN

The more we try to change people for the better, the more they stay the same. The more we try to respect them and appreciate them, to love them for their goodness as they are, the quicker they change for the better.

- RANDY COLTON ROLFE

Advice

Giving advice comes naturally to mothers. Advice is in the genes along with blue eyes and red hair.

- LOIS WYSE

The true secret of giving advice is, after you have honestly given it, to be perfectly indifferent whether it is taken or not, and never persist in trying to set people right.

- HANNAH WHITALL SMITH

Whatever advice you give, be brief.

- HORACE

Parents can only give good advice or put them on the right paths, but the final forming of a person's character lies in their own hands.

- ANNE FRANK

It is the privilege of adults to give advice. It is the privilege of youth not to listen. Both avail themselves of their privileges, and the world rocks along.

- D. SUTTON

'You know,' said Arthur, 'it's at times like this, when I'm trapped in a Vogon airlock with a man from Betelgeuse, and about to die of asphyxiation in deep space, that I really wish I'd listened to what my mother told me when I was young.'
'Why, what did she tell you?'
'I don't know, I didn't listen.'

- DOUGLAS ADAMS

Individuality

If a man does not keep pace with his companions, perhaps it is because he hears a different drummer. Let him step to the music which he hears, however measured or far away.

- HENRY DAVID THOREAU

It is not just a matter of seeing things differently, but of seeing different things.

- MARILYN FERGUSON

Children in a family are like flowers in a bouquet. There is always one determined to face in an opposite direction from the way the arranger desires.

- MARCELENE COX

Every human being must have a point at which he stands against culture, where he says, this is me and the damned world can go to hell.

- ROLLO MAY

Here is how to live without resentment or embarrassment in a world in which you are different from everyone else: Be indifferent to the difference.

-AL CAPP

While I am not in favor of maladjustment, I view . . . this hostility to eccentricity and controversy with grave misgiving. One looks back with dismay at the possibility of a Shakespeare perfectly adjusted to bourgeois life in Stratford, a Wesley contentedly administering a country parish, George Washington going to London to receive a barony from George III, or Abraham Lincoln prospering in Springfield with nary a concern for the preservation of the crumbling Union.

- ADLAI STEVENSON

To be [an individual] one must be a non-conformist.
- RALPH WALDO EMERSON

Integrity simply means a willingness not to violate one's identity.
- ERICH FROMM

A perfectly normal person is rare in our civilization.
- KAREN HORNEY

Nobody realizes that some people expend tremendous energy merely to be normal.
- ALBERT CAMUS

A child develops individuality long before he develops taste.
- ERMA BOMBECK

Letting Go

Hold close with open arms.

- MARDETTE SANDERS

In an earlier stage of motherhood, when my deepest desire was to have a single, uninterrupted bath, I had no idea how tricky and delicate this letting go would be.

- ELLEN GOODMAN

The mother-child relationship is paradoxical and, in a sense, tragic. It requires the most intense love on the mother's side, yet this very love must help the child grown away from the mother, and to become fully independent.

- ERICH FROMM

The devotion of a parent to a child — the combination of protecting them and pushing them out of the nest — is the epitome of leadership.

- ALAN LOY McGINNIS

It's always been my feeling that God lends you your children until they're about eighteen years old. If you haven't made your points with them by then, it's too late.

- BETTY FORD

Childhood is a short season.

- HELEN HAYES

Children graduate to the next stage of things. . . . What shall we give them on these occasions? Imagination, a shove out and up, a blessing.

- ROBERT FULGHUM

We not only want to help pave the way for our children to come back to us, but we want to have the courage and flexibility to go to our children.

- SHARON STRASSFELD & KATHY GREEN

As parents master the difficult task of letting go, they open the door for their adult child's friendship and love.
- JEAN OKIMOTO & PHYLLIS JACKSON STEGALL

We are not trying to educate children and send them into the world as finished products — we send them forward as persons well begun.
- ANGELO BOYO

A child enters your home and makes so much noise for twenty years you can hardly stand it — then departs, leaving the house so silent you think you will go mad.
- J. A. HOLMES

There isn't a child who hasn't gone out into the brave new world who eventually doesn't return to the old homestead carrying a bundle of dirty clothes.
- ART BUCHWALD

Once you've mastered the art of driving Joan to the orthodontist at two, getting Jenny to her piano lesson at three-fifteen, picking up David at four, being at Geoffrey's ball game at four-thirty, meeting Joe on the five-fifty boat, and starting dinner somewhere in between, how do you get used to the idea that come next year, the car will simply sit in the driveway for days at a time? Once you've trained yourself to double the ingredients for every recipe you come across, how to you manage to remember that if you make the standard two meat loaves for dinner tonight, you're going to be eating leftovers till a week from Thursday?
- ANN COMBS

Selfhood begins with a walking away, and love is proved in the letting go.
- C. DAY-LEWIS

Home & Family
A Home Is . . .

'Home' is any four walls that enclose the right person.
- HELEN ROWLAND

A house is no home unless it contains food and fire for the mind as well as the body.
- MARGARET FULLER

Peace, like charity, begins at home.
- FRANKLIN D. ROOSEVELT

Home is the place there's no place like.
- CHARLES SCHULTZ

Home is not where you live but where they understand you.
- CHRISTIAN MORGENSTERN

When there is room in the heart, there is room in the house.
- DANISH PROVERB

Home is a place where, when you have to go there, they have to take you in.
- ROBERT FROST

How hard it is to escape from places! However carefully one goes, they hold you — you leave little bits of yourself fluttering on the fences, little rags and shreds of your very life.
- KATHERINE MANSFIELD

House Keeping & Home Making

A sparkling house is a fine thing if the children aren't robbed of their luster in keeping it that way.

- MARCELENE COX

Cleaning your house while your kids are still growing is like shoveling the walk before it stops snowing.

- PHYLLIS DILLER

Here's how I get the kitchen floor mopped: I let the kids wash the dishes. They end up with so much water on the floor it has to be mopped. They are learning, and my floor shines.

- B. J. FURLAN

There are three ways to get something done: do it yourself, hire someone, or forbid your kids to do it.

- MONTA CRANE

Keeping house is like threading beads on a string with no knot at the end.

- OLD SAYING

My house is clean enough to be healthy and dirty enough to be happy.

- SUE HUTH, seen on a sampler

I am and always have been an immaculate housekeeper. It's just my house that's such a mess.

- MARY ANN CAHILL

The worst thing about work in the house or home is that whatever you do is destroyed, laid waste or eaten within twenty-four hours.

- LADY KASLUCK

My husband and I have figured out a really good system about the housework: neither one of us does it.
- DOTTIE ARCHIBALD

One never notices what has been done; one can only see what remains to be done.
- MARIE CURIE

What one *has* to do usually can be done.
- ELEANOR ROOSEVELT

To keep life simple, for each task ask:
• Does it have to be done?
• Does it have to be done now?
• Can I delegate it?
• Does it have to be perfect?
• Is there a simpler way to do it?
- LA LECHE LEAGUE

I have a simple philosophy: Fill what's empty. Empty what's full. And scratch where it itches.
- ALICE ROOSEVELT LONGWORTH

One of the advantages of being disorderly is that one is constantly making exciting discoveries.
- A. A. MILNE

The whole process of homemaking which ever has been woman's special province should be looked on as an art and a profession.
- SARAH JOSEPHA HALE (19th century)

To be a housewife is . . . a difficult, a wrenching, sometimes ungrateful job if it's looked at as only a job. Regarded as a profession, it is the noblest as it is the most ancient of the catalog.
- PHYLLIS McGINLEY

Perhaps the greatest social service that can be rendered by anybody . . . is to bring up a family. But . . . there is a very general disposition to regard a married woman's work as no work at all, and to take it as a matter of course that she should not be paid for it.

- GEORGE BERNARD SHAW

No labourer in the world is expected to work for room, board, and love — except the housewife.

- LETTY COTTIN POGREBIN

Although I knew deep within me that what I am doing is important, it is not always easy to remember this living in a society which tends to value only what can be seen, measured or possessed.

- MARGLI MATTHEWS

By and large, mothers and housewives are the only workers who do not have regular time off. They are the great vacationless class.

- ANNE MORROW LINDBERGH

Even if we cannot decorate our houses the way we would really like, or keep them looking as immaculate as we think we should, we can do other things which are far more important. . . . We can try to make our homes happy places in which to live.

- CAROL BARTHOLOMEW

Mothers & Work

Too many of us are feeling much like the miller's daughter in the fairy tale *Rumpelstiltskin*. Giving up our children in order to live up to the promise that we could spin straw into gold sounded fine before our sons and daughters were born.

- LINDA BURTON, JANET DITTMER, & CHERI LOVELESS

The really dependent days are so few that you could almost miss the whole course. . . . If you wish away those three and a half years, you may spend fifty-six and a half years being nostalgic over what you missed. *That's* unhappiness.

- POLLY BERRIEN BERENDS

Fifty years from now it won't really matter what sort of house or car you have now, but the world will be a little better because you were important in the life of a child.

- LYNN MOEN

When I am all hassled about something, I always stop and ask myself what difference it will make . . . in the next ten million years, and that question always helps me to get back my perspective.

- ANNE WILSON SCHAEF

At work, you think of the children you have left at home. At home, you think of the work you've left unfinished. Such a struggle is unleashed within yourself. Your heart is rent.

- GOLDA MEIR

I repeatedly heard career women . . . say, 'What I really need is a wife.' But maybe they don't need 'wives'; maybe they need careers basically redesigned to suit workers who also care for families.

- ARLIE HOCHSCHILD

It is time to question the *entire* inflexible business model of work — the career approach that requires us to leave our family at home and dedicate ourselves to getting ahead.

- JAN FLETCHER

I completely caved in to motherhood. I didn't want to do anything else for three years.

- CANDICE BERGEN

Did anyone ever tell Toscanini or Bach that he had to choose between music and family, between art and a normal life?

- ELISABETH MANN BORGESE

Women have always worked. They have picked roots and berries, they have harvested cotton, they have sweated in rice paddies, they have written books and painted masterpieces.

- PEGGY O'MARA

The time to relax is when you don't have time for it.

- SYDNEY J. HARRIS

There is no pleasure in having nothing to do; the fun is in having lots to do and not doing it.

- MARY LITTLE

How beautiful it is to do nothing, and then rest afterward.

- SPANISH PROVERB

One of the symptoms of an approaching nervous breakdown is the belief that one's work is terribly important.

- BERTRAND RUSSELL

Being Female

Women's lives . . . are kaleidoscopes, boxes of puzzle pieces that make a whole. It works if you accept the creativity and the challenge of an improvised, unfinished quilt or the beauty of a wild garden. It works if you can hold onto the center of all the intertwining parts, the heart that turns many pieces into harmony.

- JENNIFER JAMES

Women should be able to fulfill themselves in both roles [career and motherhood] without abandoning their instincts, especially their joy in satisfactions unique to women. . . . *To be somebody, a woman does not have to be more like a man, but more of a woman.*

- CAROL MACCINI

It is at the moment when she becomes a mother that a woman first confronts the full reality of what it means to be a woman in our society.

- ANN OAKLEY

Remember, Ginger Rogers did everything Fred Astaire did, but she did it backwards and in high heels.

- FAITH WHITTLESEY, ANN RICHARDS, and others

It occurred to me when I was thirteen and wearing white gloves and Mary Janes and going to dancing school, that no one should have to dance backward all her life.

- JILL RUCKELSHAUS

The men who espoused unpopular causes may have been considered misguided, but they were rarely attacked for their morals or their masculinity. Women who did the same thing were apt to be denounced as harlots or condemned for being *unfeminine*.

- MARGARET TRUMAN

I do not wish women to have power over men; but over themselves.

- MARY WOLLSTONECRAFT (19th century)

We live in a society that dehumanizes men and renders women impotent. We need to humanize men and empower women.

- KELDUYN GARLAND

When self-respect takes its rightful place in the psyche of woman, she will not allow herself to be manipulated by anyone.

- INDIRA MAHINDRA

True female self-esteem comes not from being just like men but enjoying the differences.

- NILES NEWTON

When she stopped conforming to the conventional picture of femininity she finally began to enjoy being a woman.

- BETTY FRIEDAN

A woman is the full circle. Within her is the power to create, nurture, and transform. A woman knows that nothing can be born without darkness and nothing can come to fruition without light.

- DIANE MARIECHILD

Take your life in your own hands, and what happens? A terrible thing: no one to blame.

- ERICA JONG

Families & Society

In any society the way a woman gives birth and the kind of care given to her and the baby point as sharply as an arrowhead to the key values in the culture.

- SHEILA KITZINGER

It is a comment on our times that we who want childbirth to again become an intimate family affair are considered radicals.

- DORIS HAIRE

No one raises a child alone. Parents who assume that this is possible find themselves entrapped by loneliness and fatigue, and their children are all the more vulnerable to influences beyond their families.

- RICHARD LOUV

It takes a village to raise a child.

- AFRICAN PROVERB

How much better off were [the] mothers, grandmothers, and great-grandmothers who lived in extended families with extra arms to hug a needy child and extra ears to listen to her complaints?

- EVELYN BASSOFF

Could I climb to the highest place in Athens, I would lift my voice and proclaim, 'Fellow citizens, why do you turn and scrape every stone to gather wealth and take so little care of your children to whom one day you must relinquish it all.'

- SOCRATES (about 420 B.C.)

If we don't find a way to prevent the painful abandonment, abuse and exploitation of children, we will spend the rest of our lives building mental hospitals and prisons.

- KARL MENNINGER

Child-rearing is the most difficult task that most ordinary mortals will ever undertake. It is the first priority of this and every nation, costly to do well and costlier to neglect.
- E. JAMES LIEBERMAN

Our society has not done well institutionalizing our old, our sick, or our mentally ill. Why do we think we will do any better institutionalizing our children?
- NILES NEWTON

As a society, we love children only when they are *under control*. We hate children who defy us. We fear children who want democracy for themselves, children who are independent, quirky, free-thinking, nonconformist, idiosyncratic, superior, or critical of adults.
- LETTY COTTIN POGREBIN

What's done to children, they will do to society.
- KARL MENNINGER

The motherhood role is one society encourages a woman to take, but once she does, society leaves her alone. Furthermore, it blames her for every possible problem her child may have and even excuses adult behavior on the grounds of faulty mothering.
- BOSTON WOMEN'S HEALTH BOOK COLLECTIVE

We shouldn't . . . assume all of our problems, all the conflicts of family life, come from within us. . . . Much of our stress is the result of living in communities that are not responsive to the needs of the people who live in them.
- RANDY MEYERS WOLFSON & VIRGINIA DELUCA

Never doubt that a small group of thoughtful, committed citizens can change the world. Indeed, it is the only thing that ever has.
- MARGARET MEAD

Mother Earth

The control man has secured over nature has far outrun his control over himself.

- ERNEST JONES

We are the curators of life on earth; we hold it in the palms of our hands.

- HELEN CALDICOTT

Late on the third day, at the very moment when, at sunset . . . there flashed upon my mind unforseen and unsought, the phrase, *Reverence for Life.*

- ALBERT SCHWEITZER

Today the planet is so small that the fate of all humankind is intertwined. . . . As individuals we must see ourselves as parts of a single organism.

- JONAS SALK

Human beings are designed . . . to grow and develop in cooperation, and the future development of humanity lies . . . with increasing love extended to all creatures everywhere . . . for without love there can be no healthy development, no real life.

- ASHLEY MONTAGU

Babies are necessary to grown-ups. . . . In a world that is cutting down trees to build highways, losing its earth to concrete, babies are almost the only remaining link with nature, with the natural world of living things from which we spring.

- EDA LeSHAN

We didn't inherit the land from our fathers. We are borrowing it from our children.

- AMISH BELIEF

Anger

Anger is neither legitimate nor illegitimate, meaningful nor pointless. Anger simply is.
- HARRIET GOLDHOR LERNER

Anger is a defense mechanism. You are defensive because you are frightened.
- LOUISE HAY

The best remedy for a short temper is a long walk.
- JACQELINE SCHIFF

If you are patient in one moment of anger, you will escape a hundred days of sorrow.
- CHINESE PROVERB

How much more grievous are the consequences of anger than the causes of it.
- MARCUS AURELIUS (2nd century A.D.)

We really love our neighbor as ourselves: We do unto others as we do unto ourselves. . . . It is not love of self but hatred of self which is at the root of the troubles that afflict our world.
- ERIC HOFFER

If you hate a person, you hate something in him that is part of yourself. What isn't part of ourselves doesn't disturb us.
- HERMANN HESSE

If there be trouble, let it be in my day, that my children may have peace.
- THOMAS PAINE

The time not to become a father is eighteen years before a war.
- E. B. WHITE

Happiness is not the absence of conflict but the ability to cope with it.

- OLD SAYING

Honest differences are often a healthy sign of progress.

- MAHATMA GANDHI

Perseverance is more prevailing than violence; and many things which cannot be overcome when they are together, yield themselves up when taken little by little.

- PLUTARCH (late first century A.D.)

Man must evolve for all human conflict a method which rejects revenge, aggression and retaliation. The foundation of such a method is love.

- MARTIN LUTHER KING, Jr.

The remedy for wrongs is to forget them.

- PUBLILIUS SYRUS

Always forgive your enemies — nothing annoys them so much.

- OSCAR WILDE

You can no more win a war than you can win an earthquake.

- JEANNETTE RANKIN

I dream of giving birth to a child who will ask, 'Mother, what was war?'

- EVE MERRIAM

Mankind must remember that peace is not God's gift to his creatures; peace is our gift to each other.

- ELIE WIESEL

First keep the peace within yourself, then you can also bring peace to others.

- THOMAS à KEMPIS (15th century)

A Family Is . . .

Whether by choice or circumstance, families come in all shapes and sizes. And ultimately, what really defines a family is commitment, caring and love.

- CANDICE BERGEN

Other things may change us, but we start and end with family.

- ANTHONY BRANDT

Family faces are magic mirrors. Looking at people who belong to us, we see the past, present, and future.

- GAIL LUMET BUCKLEY

What families have in common the world around is that they are the place where people learn who they are and how to be that way.

- JEAN ILLSLEY CLARKE

Call it a clan, call it a network, call it a tribe, call it a family. Whatever you call it, whoever you are, you need one.

- JANE HOWARD

Family means everyone who loves and cares for you, and whom you love and care for in return. And the most meaningful values within that caring group of people are respect, responsibility, and love and emotional support.

- LEE SALK

Men, women, and children still function best living in cooperative, loving relationships with close physical interaction. Our society does not make this easy.

- NILES NEWTON

Good family life is never an accident but always an achievement by those who share it.

- JAMES H. S. BOSSARD

If families are to become strong again, it is not going to be done by professionals but by individuals within . . . their own families, each working to make his or her own family a better and more loving unit.

- NILES NEWTON

Parenting, at its best, comes as naturally as laughter. It is automatic, involuntary, unconditional love.

- SALLY JAMES

To maintain a joyful family requires much from both the parents and the children. Each member of the family has to become, in a special way, the servant of the others.

- POPE JOHN PAUL II

Each of us is special and unique in the universe and . . . love is the most powerful device that we have in our lives.

- WAYNE DYER

I believe in loving and being loved . . . without loving and being loved, the human soul and spirit would curdle and die.

- VIRGINIA SATIR

Words spoken kindly are not enough. If there is no energy of love from the heart, the child wilts. It is in the radiance of love that all people, especially children, blossom into a being of beauty and excellence.

- JEAN ARMON

Healthy families are our greatest national resource.

- DOLORES CURRAN

Family Love

Little children are still the symbol of the eternal marriage between love and duty.

- GEORGE ELIOT

Four hugs a day are necessary for survival, eight are good for maintenance, and twelve for growth.

- VIRGINIA SATIR

I do not love him because he is good, but because he is my little child.

- RABINDRANATH TAGORE

The ultimate lesson all of us have to learn is *unconditional love*, which includes not only others but ourselves as well.

- ELISABETH KÜBLER-ROSS

Unconditional love does not mean liking everything a loved one does.

- PEGGY O'MARA

I Love You No Matter What You Do, But Do You Have to Do So Much of It?

- JEAN ILLSLEY CLARKE (chapter title)

Loving a child doesn't mean giving in to all his whims; to love him is to bring out the best in him, to teach him to love what is difficult.

- NADIA BOULANGER

Sometimes one of my children will put silky arms around my neck and stare deep into my eyes . . . and say with full force of heart 'I love you'. . . . My first reaction is to be drowned in happiness. My second is to think: Don't mean it so much. Don't feel it so deeply. Don't let me have so much influence over you. Of course, I have no choice. And neither do they.

- ANNA QUINDLEN

Continuity & Generations

Patterns of the past echo in the present and resound through the future.

- DHYANI YWAHOO

A child is proof of the future, evidence that it does not end with this.

- SHEILA KITZINGER

Our children are not going to be just our children — they are going to be other people's husbands and wives and the parents of our grandchildren.

- MARY S. CALDERONE

Plants bear witness to the reality of roots.

- MOSES MAIMONIDES

Children are a kind of confirmation of life. The only form of immortality that we can be sure of.

- PETER USTINOV

The events in our lives happen in a sequence in time, but in their significance to ourselves, they find their own order . . . the continuous thread of revelation.

- EUDORA WELTY

Once you have a child you stop thinking in terms of your lifespan only.

- PAT BENATAR

Paradoxically, it is the knowledge of our imminent death — that we are the next in line — that moves us to treasure our aliveness and realize our beautiful possibilities.

- EVELYN BASSOFF

We are always in the process of designing our descendants.

- WILLARD GAYLIN

I don't know who my grandfather was, but I am much more concerned to know what his grandson will be.

- ABRAHAM LINCOLN

My daughter bore a son and became a mother, while I became a grandmother and my mother became a great-grandmother. . . . I can continue on my way knowing that those behind me can follow, . . . and I go on with a happy heart and thankfulness.

- MARIE TAYOUMANA LEVY

Slowly it dawned on me that to be born and to give birth are one and the same; that the very act of giving birth takes a woman back to the moment of her own birth.

- YVONNE FITZGERALD

I believe the child should be taught from the very first that the whole world is his world, that adult and child share one world, that all generations are needed.

- PEARL S. BUCK

Grandparents & Grandchildren

It is as grandmothers that our mothers come into the fullness of their grace.

- CHRISTOPHER MORLEY

Because [grandparents] are usually free to love and guide and befriend the young without having to take daily responsibility for them, they can often reach out past pride and fear of failure and close the space between generations.

- JIMMY CARTER

It is, of course, our grandparents who are instrumental in handing down the culture, in transmitting the traditions down to the new generation.

- SELMA WASSERMANN

No matter how grandparents act, they affect the emotional well-being of their grandchildren, for better or for worse, simply because they exist.

- ARTHUR KORNHABER

Most grandparents . . . try hard not to interfere. On the other hand, they have had experience, they feel they've developed judgment, they love their grandchildren dearly, and they can't help having opinions.

- BENJAMIN SPOCK

After a long adolescence and early womanhood of having very little in common with your mother, you may find the baby is a marvelous source of mutual interest and love.

- PADDY O'BRIEN

Grandchildren are the dots that connect the lines from generation to generation.

- LOIS WYSE

It is one of nature's ways that we often feel closer to distant generations than to the generation immediately preceding us.

- IGOR STRAVINSKY

No matter how old a mother is, she watches her middle-aged children for signs of improvement.

- FLORIDA SCOTT-MAXWELL

One of the mysteries of life is how the boy who wasn't good enough to marry the daughter can be the father of the smartest grandchild in the world.

- ARMCHAIR PHILOSOPHER

A mother becomes a true grandmother the day she stops noticing the terrible things her children do because she is so enchanted with the wonderful things her grandchildren do.

- LOIS WYSE

Nothing makes a boy smarter than being a grandson.

- OLD SAYING

Our grandchildren accept us for ourselves . . . as no one else in our entire lives has ever done, not our parents, siblings, spouses, friends — and hardly ever our own grown children.

- RUTH GOODE

There is a sense of the eternal in reading or singing or telling the same story to my granddaughter that my own child enjoyed.

- NANCY BUCKINGHAM

Grandparents and grandchildren do not have to *do* anything to make each other happy. Their happiness comes from *being* together.

- ARTHUR KORNHABER

To clasp the small, trusting hand of my grandchild and to have her look at me with delight, faith, and total openness and acceptance gives a joy that I didn't take enough time to savor the first time around.

- NANCY BUCKINGHAM

A grandmother will put a sweater on you when she is cold, feed you when she is hungry, and put you to bed when she is tired.

- ERMA BOMBECK

I don't go along with all this talk of a generation gap. We're all contemporaries. There is only a difference in memories, that's all.

- W. H. AUDEN

Grandchildren are indeed the greatest. . . . You can have them when you want them — if you behave yourself reasonably well with their parents. And you can always take them back home when you're tired.

- STELLA CHESS & JANE WHITBREAD

By the time the youngest children have learned to keep the house tidy, the oldest grandchildren are on hand to tear it to pieces.

- CHRISTOPHER MORLEY

Grandparents are our continuing tie to the near-past, to the events and beliefs and experiences that so strongly affect our lives and the world around us.

- JIMMY CARTER

Grandparents are for telling you what it used to be like, but not too much.

- CHARLES SHEDD

If the very old will remember, the very young will listen.
- CHIEF DAN GEORGE

Life
The Quality of Life

To every thing there is a season,
And a time to every purpose under the heaven:
A time to be born, and a time to die;
A time to plant, and a time to pluck up that which is
planted . . .
A time to get, and a time to lose;
A time to keep, and a time to cast away . . .
A time to love, and a time to hate;
A time of war, and a time of peace.

- ECCLESIASTES 3:1-8

There is a beginning and an ending for everything that is
alive. In between is living.

- BRYAN MELLONIE & ROBERT INGPEN

Life was meant to be lived and curiosity must be kept
alive. One must never, for whatever reason, turn his back
on life.

- ELEANOR ROOSEVELT

People say that what we're all seeking is a meaning for
life. . . . I think that what we're seeking is an experience of
being alive.

- JOSEPH CAMPBELL

I don't want to get to the end of my life and find that I
just lived the length of it. I want to have lived the width
of it as well.

- DIANE ACKERMAN

I have spent my days stringing and unstringing my
instrument while the song I came to sing remains
unsung.

- RABINDRANATH TAGORE

You don't get to choose how you're going to die. Or when. You can decide how you're going to live. Now.

- JOAN BAEZ

Stop Improving Yourself and START LIVING.

- ROBERTA JEAN BRYANT (book title)

The greater part of your happiness or misery will depend on your disposition and not your circumstances.

- MARTHA WASHINGTON

It is never too late to be what you might have been.

- GEORGE ELIOT

Enjoy your ice cream while it's on your plate — that's my philosophy.

- THORNTON WILDER

Treat yourself at least as well as you treat other people.

- THEODORE RUBIN

To live fully, we must learn to use things and love people.

- JOHN POWELL

What a wonderful life I've had! I only wish I'd realized it sooner.

- COLETTE

Life is what happens to us while we are making other plans.

-THOMAS la MANCE

Death is not the greatest loss in life. The greatest loss is what dies inside us while we live.

- NORMAN COUSINS

When you have only two pennies left in the world, buy a loaf of bread with one, and a lily with the other.

- CHINESE PROVERB

Moderation

We are all dreaming of some magical rose garden over the horizon instead of enjoying the roses that are blooming outside our windows today.

- DALE CARNEGIE

We do not remember days, we remember moments.

- CESARE PAVESE

The real art of living is beginning where you are.

- UNKNOWN

There must be more to life than having everything.

- MAURICE SENDAK

Perhaps too much of everything is as bad as too little.

- EDNA FERBER

He who is content always has enough.

- CHINESE PROVERB

One cannot collect all the beautiful shells on the beach. One can collect only a few, and they are more beautiful if they are few.

- ANNE MORROW LINDBERGH

To be without some of the things you want is an indispensable part of happiness.

- BERTRAND RUSSELL

The really happy man is the one who can enjoy the scenery even when he has a detour.

- OLD SAYING

Sun & Shadow

There is no sun without shadow, and it is essential to know the night.

- ALBERT CAMUS

To light a candle is to cast a shadow.

- URSULA K. LeGUIN

There are as many nights as days, and the one is just as long as the other in the year's course. Even a happy life cannot be without a measure of darkness, and the word 'happy' would lose its meaning if it were not balanced by sadness.

- CARL JUNG

We could never learn to be brave and patient, if there were only joy in the world.

- HELEN KELLER

Life is an onion. You peel it off one layer at a time, and sometimes you weep.

- CARL SANDBURG

The cure for anything is salt water — sweat, tears, or the sea.

- ISAK DINESEN

Life itself is the test and there is no end to the testing as long as the person breathes.

- MURSHIDA VERA JUSTIN CORDA

The human spirit is virtually indestructible and its ability to rise from the ashes remains as long as the body draws breath.

- ALICE MILLER

Giving

You give little when you give of your possessions. It is when you give of yourself that you truly give.

- KAHLIL GIBRAN

We make a living by what we get, but we make a life by what we give.

- WINSTON CHURCHILL

You are of more use to society if you use your rarest gifts.

- EDWARD RUMELY

One needs something to believe in, something for which one can have whole-hearted enthusiasm. One needs to feel that one's life has meaning, that one is needed in this world.

- HANNAH SENESH

So long as we love, we serve; so long as we are loved by others, I would almost say that we are indispensable; and no man is useless while he has a friend.

- ROBERT LOUIS STEVENSON

Do something for somebody every day for which you do not get paid.

- ALBERT SCHWEITZER

No person was ever honored for what he received. Honor has been the reward for what he gave.

- CALVIN COOLIDGE

Real joy comes not from ease or riches or from the praise of men, but from doing something worthwhile.

- SIR WILFRED T. GRENFELL

Risks & Courage

Everyone has talent. What is rare is the courage to follow the talent to the dark place where it leads.

- ERICA JONG

We all have greater powers than we think. . . . Whatever we want to learn or learn to do, we probably can learn. . . Our lives and our possibilities are not fixed by what happened to us when we were little or by what experts say we can or cannot do.

- JOHN HOLT

Ah, but a man's reach should exceed his grasp, or what's a heaven for?

- ROBERT BROWNING

Whatever you can do, or dream you can, begin it. Boldness has genius, power and magic in it.

- JOHANN WOLFGANG VON GOETHE

You can aim for what you want and if you don't get it, you don't get it; but if you don't aim, you don't get anything.

- FRANCINE PROSE

While one person hesitates because he feels inferior, the other is busy making mistakes and becoming superior.

- HENRY C. LINK

You gain strength, courage and confidence by every experience in which you really stop to look fear in the face.

- ELEANOR ROOSEVELT

If you're never scared or embarrassed or hurt, it means you never take any chances.

- JULIA SOREL

In great attempts it is glorious even to fail.

- OLD SAYING

Life is either a daring adventure or nothing. To keep our faces toward change and behave like free spirits in the presence of fate is strength undefeatable.

- HELEN KELLER

Worry is like a rocking chair — it gives you something to do but it doesn't get you anywhere.

- DOROTHY GALYEAN

You can't start worrying about what's going to happen. You get spastic enough worrying about what's happening now.

- LAUREN BACALL

This art of resting the mind and the power of dismissing from it all care and worry is probably one of the secrets of energy in our great men.

- J. A. HADFIELD

There is only one way to happiness and that is to cease worrying about things which are beyond the power of our will.

- EPICTETUS

The way I see it, if you want the rainbow, you gotta put up with the rain.

- DOLLY PARTON

Don't be afraid to take a big step if one is indicated. You can't cross a chasm in two small jumps.

- DAVID LLOYD GEORGE

I am an old man and have known a great many troubles, but most of them have never happened.

- MARK TWAIN

Security does not exist in nature, nor do the children of men as a whole experience it. Avoiding danger is no safer in the long run than exposure.

- HELEN KELLER

If you wait for tomorrow, tomorrow comes. If you don't wait for tomorrow, tomorrow comes.

- SENEGALESE PROVERB

The only courage that matters is the kind that gets you from one minute to the next.

- MIGNON McLAUGHLIN

Courage is resistance to fear, mastery of fear — *not* absence of fear.

- MARK TWAIN

The fishermen know that the sea is dangerous and the storm terrible, but they have never found these dangers sufficient reason for remaining ashore.

- VINCENT VAN GOGH

Accept that all of us can be hurt, that all of us can — and surely will at times — fail. . . . I think we should follow a simple rule: if we can take the worst, take the risk.

- JOYCE BROTHERS

And the trouble is, if you don't risk anything, you risk even *more*.

- ERICA JONG

Once a decision was made, I did not worry about it afterward.

- HARRY S. TRUMAN

You must do the thing you think you cannot do.

- ELEANOR ROOSEVELT

Change & Crisis

God, grant me the serenity to accept the things I cannot change, courage to change the things I can, and wisdom to know the difference.

- REINHOLD NIEBUHR

All is flux, nothing stays still. . . . Nothing endures but change.

- HERACLITUS (5th century B.C.)

When we reach one conclusion we only become part of another beginning.

- PAULA D'ARCY

When one door closes, another opens; but we often look so long and so regretfully upon the closed door that we do not see the one which has opened for us.

- ALEXANDER GRAHAM BELL

The greatest discovery of my generation is that a human being can alter his life by altering his attitude.

- WILLIAM JAMES

Be the change you hope to see.

- MAHATMA GANDHI

Not everything that is faced can be changed, but nothing can be changed until it is faced.

- GEORGE BALDWIN

Every problem has in it the seeds of its own solution. If you don't have any problems, you don't get any seeds.

- NORMAN VINCENT PEALE

That is what learning is. You suddenly understand something you've understood all your life, but in a new way.

- DORIS LESSING

Don't let life discourage you; everyone who got where he is had to begin where he was.

- RICHARD L. EVANS

The word 'crisis,' when written in Chinese, is composed of two characters: one represents danger, the other, opportunity.

- VIRGINIA LAWRENCE LARSEN

You can't afford to make life into more of a crisis than it already is. Try to keep it all in perspective.

- DORIS JASINEK & PAMELA BELL RYAN

If you have made mistakes, even serious ones, there is always another chance for you. What we call failure is not the falling down, but the staying down.

- MARY PICKFORD

When you get into a tight place and everything goes against you, till it seems as though you could not hang on a minute longer, never give up then, for that is just the place and time that the tide will turn.

- HARRIET BEECHER STOWE (19th century)

Birds sing after a storm; why shouldn't people feel as free to delight in whatever remains to them?

- ROSE FITZGERALD KENNEDY

At fifteen life had taught me undeniably that surrender, in its place, was as honorable as resistance, especially if one had no choice.

- MAYA ANGELOU

The world breaks everyone and afterwards many are strong in the broken places.

- ERNEST HEMINGWAY

Grieving

Ours is a death-denying culture. In denying death we often deny the needs of those who are touched by death and sometimes even the existence of those who were so briefly with us and then died.
- CLAUDIA PANUTHOS & CATHERINE ROMEO

When your parent dies you've lost your past but when your child dies you've lost your future.
- OLD SAYING

A person's a person no matter how small.
- DR. SEUSS

I miss you, although I did not know you. I wanted you but I could not have you. I cry for you silently. . . . I just can't forget you.
- Woman who had a miscarriage

What we hold in our hearts, we can never lose, and all that we love deeply becomes a part of us.
- HELEN KELLER

She needs to cry like her soul was ripped apart because it was.
- JEANNE WATSON DRISCOLL

Weeping is only a stage; it won't last forever. You needn't be afraid to cry.
- ALLA RENÉE BOZARTH-CAMPBELL

And ever has it been that love knows not its own depth until the hour of separation.
- KAHLIL GIBRAN

Crying is not the pain. . . . Life is the pain. Crying is the discharge of the pain. Crying is the healing of the pain.
- ROBERT MARK ALTER

Pain nourishes courage. You can't be brave if you've only had wonderful things happen to you.

- MARY TYLER MOORE

It isn't for the moment you are struck that you need courage, but for the long uphill climb back to sanity and faith and security.

- ANNE MORROW LINDBERGH

Never does one feel oneself so utterly helpless as in trying to speak comfort for great bereavement.

- JANE WELSH CARLYLE (1853)

Grief can't be shared. Everyone carries it alone, his own burden, his own way.

- ANNE MORROW LINDBERGH

I'll love you forever, I'll like you for always,
As long as I'm living my baby you'll be.

- ROBERT MUNSCH

We say we cannot bear our troubles but when we get to them we bear them.

- NING LAO T'AI-T'AI

Sometimes the Lord calms the storm; sometimes He lets the storm rage, and calms His child.

- OLD SAYING

Trouble is a tunnel through which we must pass and not a brick wall against which we must break our head.

- PROVERB

Expecting life to treat you well because you are a good person is like expecting an angry bull not to charge because you are a vegetarian.

- SHARI R. BARR

The question of why bad things happen to good people translates itself into some very different questions, . . . asking how we will respond, and what we intend to do now that it has happened.

- HAROLD KUSHNER

No one ever told me that grief felt so like fear.

- C. S. LEWIS

We are healed of a suffering only by experiencing it to the full.

- MARCEL PROUST

You cannot stop the birds of sadness from flying over your head, but you can prevent them from nesting in your hair.

- CHINESE PROVERB

Profound joy of the heart is like a magnet that indicates the path of life. One has to follow it, even though one enters into a way full of difficulties.

- MOTHER TERESA

I haven't a clue as to how my story will end. But that's all right. When you set out on a journey and night covers the road, you don't conclude that the road has vanished. And how else could we discover the stars?

- NANCY WILLARD

Authenticity

An atmosphere of trust, love, and humor can nourish extraordinary human capacity. One key is authenticity: parents acting as people, not as roles.

- MARILYN FERGUSON

Don't compromise yourself. You are all you've got.

- JANIS JOPLIN

The least useful thing I can do for those I love is to save them from their own pain. When I try to rescue or protect them from the full realization of their own truths or solve their problems for them, I weaken their initiative and confidence. When they are allowed to make their own mistakes, they learn valuable lessons.

- ROBERTA JEAN BRYANT

A 'no' uttered from the deepest conviction is better and greater than a 'yes' merely uttered to please, or what is worse, to avoid trouble.

- MAHATMA GANDHI

We know the truth, not only by the reason, but by the heart

.- BLAISE PASCAL

The truth is more important than facts.

- FRANK LLOYD WRIGHT

Always speak the truth and you'll never be concerned with your memory.

- OLD SAYING

Love truth, but pardon error.

- FRANÇOIS MARIE AROUET DE VOLTAIRE

It wasn't until quite late in life that I discovered how easy it is to say, 'I don't know.'

- W. SOMERSET MAUGHAM

It is not easy to find happiness in ourselves, and it is not possible to find it elsewhere.

- AGNES REPPLIER

'If you always do what interests you, then at least one person is pleased.'

- KATHARINE HEPBURN (advice from her mother)

I cannot give you the formula for success, but I can give you the formula for failure — which is: Try to please everybody.

- HERBERT BAYARD SWOPE

I also know that when I'm trusting and being myself as fully as possible, everything in my life reflects this by falling into place easily, often miraculously.

- SHAKTI GAWAIN

We must not allow other people's limited perceptions to define us.

- VIRGINIA SATIR

One is taught by experience to put a premium on those few people who can appreciate you for what you are.

- GAIL GODWIN

The most exhausting thing in life, I have discovered, is being insincere. That is why so much social life is exhausting; one is wearing a mask.

- ANNE MORROW LINDBERGH

Occasionally a product comes out in a 'New and Improved' version; usually I don't like it as well. The older I get the less I want to be new and improved. More and more I seek simply to risk being fully who I am.

- ROBERTA JEAN BRYANT

Mature Love & Marriage

As a young girl, I dreamed of falling into a great love. . . .
Now, as a middle-aged woman, . . . I [have] a great love
— not one *fallen into*, however, but one *earned* through
twenty-two years of living in an atmosphere of mutual
kindness and respect.

- EVELYN BASSOFF

I would like to have engraved inside every wedding
band, 'Be kind to one another.' This is . . . the secret of
making love last through the years.

- RANDOLPH RAY

Relationships . . . are not easy. . . . Even though some
relationships may appear drought resistant or
weatherproof, these qualities do not 'just happen.'

- PEGGY O'MARA

Love doesn't just sit there, like a stone, it has to be made,
like bread; remade all the time, made new.

- URSULA LeGUIN

And someday there shall be such closeness that when
one cries the other shall taste salt.

- UNKNOWN

Married love is best expressed through small acts: a
caring word when the other feels blue, . . . a little gift for
no reason, a good laugh at a shared joke, an embrace.

- EVELYN BASSOFF

Sexiness wears thin after a while and beauty fades, but to
be married to a man who makes you laugh every day, ah,
now that's a real treat!

- JOANNE WOODWARD

Your breasts are baby-chewed, your belly shows stretch marks — your decorations of honor, Adorable One. Of valor. They make you *more* beautiful. So stand straight and tall, my lovely, and forget about silver hairs. Be what you *are*, and be it in style!

- ROBERT A. HEINLEIN

Mature love, unlike early love, is tolerant of imperfection. It values human ordinariness, that mixture of strengths and shortcomings that is each of us.

- EVELYN BASSOFF

We must be our own before we can be another's.

- RALPH WALDO EMERSON

Perhaps the greatest blessing in marriage is that it lasts so long. . . . In a series of temporary relationships, one misses the ripening, gathering, harvesting joys, the deep, hard-won truths of marriage.

- RICHARD C. CABOT

A lady of 47 who has been married 27 years and has six children knows what love really is and once described it for me like this: 'Love is what you've been through with somebody.'

- JAMES THURBER

Respect . . . is appreciation of the separateness of the other person, of the ways in which he or she is unique.

- ANNIE GOTTLIEB

Treasure each other in the recognition that we do not know how long we shall have each other.

- JOSHUA LIEBMAN

Middle Years

The great thing about getting older is that you don't lose all the other ages you've been.

- MADELINE L'ENGLE

What an advantage we have over our children! While they, to their embarrassment, grow up — voices changing, legs and arms becoming too obvious . . . we gracefully, comfortably, grow down.

- JOYCE KILMER

After a certain number of years, our faces become our biographies.

- CYNTHIA OZICK

The best cosmetic in the world is an active mind that is always finding something new.

- MARY MEEK ATKESON

A half-century of living should put a good deal into a woman's face besides a few wrinkles and some unwelcome folds around the chin.

- FRANCES PARKINSON KEYES

Middle age is when you've met so many people that every new person you meet reminds you of someone else.

- OGDEN NASH

One of the many things nobody ever tells you about middle age is that it's such a nice change from being young.

- DOROTHY CANFIELD FISHER

The most creative force in the world is the menopausal woman with zest.

- MARGARET MEAD

After a woman passes menopause she really comes into her time. I feel that. I've never felt so well or had so many images before me.

- MERIDEL LeSUEUR

Hot flashes are really just power surges.

- LASSIE WITTMAN

Something very special happens to women when they know that they will not have a child — or any more children. . . . Suddenly, their whole creativity is released.

- MARGARET MEAD

What I want to do is draw middle-aged women out of their purdah, make them really joyous. . . . This is the time when everything comes good for you — your humor, your style, your bad temper.

- GERMAINE GREER

Women may be the one group that grows more radical with age.

- GLORIA STEINEM

Time and trouble will tame an advanced young woman, but an advanced old woman is uncontrollable by any earthly force.

- DOROTHY L. SAYERS

Being young is beautiful, but being old is comfortable.

- MARIE VON EBNER-ESCHENBACH

When men reach their sixties and retire, they go to pieces. Women go right on cooking.

- GAIL SHEEHY

Wisdom

Wisdom doesn't automatically come with old age.
Nothing does — except wrinkles. It's true, some wines
improve with age. But only if the grapes were good in
the first place.

- ABIGAIL VAN BUREN

Kindness is more important than wisdom, and the
recognition of this is the beginning of wisdom.

- THEODORE ISAAC RUBIN

Pain makes man think. Thought makes man wise.
Wisdom makes life endurable.

- JOHN PATRICK

An optimist is a person who sees a green light
everywhere. The pessimist sees only the red light. But
the truly wise person is color blind.

- ALBERT SCHWEITZER

A truly wise man knows how little he really knows.

- OLD SAYING

Wisdom is the reward you get for a lifetime of listening
when you'd have preferred to talk.

- DOUG LARSON

There are two statements about human beings that are
true: that all human beings are alike, and that all are
different. On those two facts all human wisdom is
founded.

- MARK VAN DOREN

Growing Old

I am not young enough to know everything.

- J.M. BARRIE

The excitement of learning separates youth from old age. As long as you're learning, you're not old.

- ROSLYN S. YALOW

Learning is ever young, even in old age.

-AESCHYLUS, 4th century BC

We do not stop playing because we are old. We grow old because we stop playing.

- OLD SAYING

Learning from their children is the best opportunity most people have to assure a meaningful old age.

- M. SCOTT PECK

Iron rusts from disuse; stagnant water loses its purity and in cold weather becomes frozen; even so does inaction sap the vigor of the mind.

- LEONARDO da VINCI (15th century)

Senility doesn't come from old age — it comes from not being loved and not being useful. As long as you feel useful, you'll never grow old.

- LEO BUSCAGLIA

Loneliness and the feeling of being unwanted is the most terrible poverty.

- MOTHER TERESA

My formula for youth: Keep your enthusiasms and forget your birthdays.

- ARMCHAIR PHILOSOPHER

One can remain alive long past the usual date of disintegration if one is unafraid of change, insatiable in intellectual curiosity, interested in big things, and happy in small ways.

- EDITH WHARTON

If you love the things you do, you don't age, you always remain young. Age is for the calendar.

- SOL HUROK

One thing is certain, and I have always known it — the joys of my life have nothing to do with age.

- MAY SARTON

Age is strictly a case of mind over matter. If you don't mind, it doesn't matter.

- JACK BENNY

Growing old is no more than a bad habit which a busy man has no time for.

- ANDRÉ MAUROIS

To me, old age is always fifteen years older than I am.
- BERNARD M. BARUCH (on his 85th birthday)

Sure, I'm for helping the elderly. I'm going to be old myself someday.

- LILLIAN CARTER (in her eighties)

Ah, well, perhaps one has to be very old before one learns how to be amused rather than shocked.

- PEARL S. BUCK

We grow neither better or worse as we get old, but more like ourselves.

- MARY LAMBERTON BECKER

The main thing in life is not to be afraid to be human.
- PABLO CASALS

Though it sounds absurd, it is true to say I felt younger at sixty than I had felt at twenty.

- ELLEN GLASGOW

The hardest years in life are those between ten and seventy.

- HELEN HAYES

Old age isn't so bad when you consider the alternative.

- MAURICE CHEVALIER

Neither for men nor for women do we anywhere find initiation ceremonies that confirm the status of being an elder.

- SIMONE de BEAUVOIR

When I was young, my parents told me what to do; now that I am old, my children tell me what to do. I wonder when I will be able to do what I want to do.

-OLD SAYING

Everyone wants to live long, but no one wants to grow old, for old age, as someone has aptly put it, is a dirty trick. The answer to that, of course, is to die young — as late as possible.

- ASHLEY MONTAGU

Whom the gods love die young, no matter how long they live.

- ELBERT HUBBARD

She had finally reached the age where she was more afraid of getting old than dying.

- JULIA PHILLIPS

The Circle Closes – Death & Dying

They say such nice things about people at their funerals
that it makes me sad to realize that I'm going to miss
mine by just a few days.

- GARRISON KEILLOR

Death is simply a shedding of the physical body, like the
butterfly coming out of a cocoon. . . . It's like putting
away your winter coat when spring comes.

- ELISABETH KÜBLER-ROSS

Dying is a wild night and a new road.

- EMILY DICKINSON (19th century)

No one should ever cry alone. No one should ever die
alone.

- LEO BUSCAGLIA

Everybody is born once and everybody dies once — it's
really the only thing we all do. It's pain and joy and
sensual and aggressive and ecstacy all in one. And who
can say whether it hurts or it is exquisite pleasure at that
moment?

- RAVEN LANG

The life of a man is a circle from childhood to childhood
and so it is in everything where power moves.

- BLACK ELK

Out of life comes death and out of death, life.
Out of the young, the old, and out of the old, the young.
Out of waking, sleep, and out of sleep, waking.
The stream of creation and dissolution never stops.

- HERACLITUS

Death belongs to life as birth does. The walk is in the
raising of the foot as in the laying of it down.

- RABINDRANATH TAGORE

About the Authors

Lynn Moen is the former owner/manager of The Birth & Life Bookstore (1980-1993). Through Birth & Life, she offered the best of the available books on pregnancy, birth, breastfeeding, child care, women's and children's health, life and love, and related issues for both professionals and the general public. Before opening Birth & Life, she started and managed the ICEA (International Childbirth Education Association) Bookcenter (1964-1980). Lynn was also the first La Leche League leader in Washington State (1964) and was named a "Living Treasure" by Mothering Magazine in 2000. After "retiring," she worked with authors to edit and nurture them through the process of bringing their books to publication. Now she is writing her memoirs and family history.

Judy Laik was co-editor with Lynn for the Birth & Life Bookstore's newsletter/catalog, *Imprints* and also reviewed books for the *Imprints*. After Lynn sold the store, Judy continued for awhile to review books for the store's new owner. She has had a children's book and a story in a historical anthology for middle-grade children published; as well as two historical romances written as Judith Laik. She is working on other historical romances and young adult novels. She also writes articles on promotion for writers for 1st Turning Point.
http://1stturningpoint.com
Her website is http://www.judithlaik.com

Learn more about the authors and *Around the Circle Gently* at:
aroundthecirclegently.com

Index

A

C